S0-BZO-361

generosity-
GENROZT

(n) "a gracious act that creates a joyful ache
every time it is remembered"

Memories of Generosities and Gratitude
including reflections by 29 scholars of
Our Lady of Destiny Catholic School

Stephen M. Kahnert
Generosity Coach

Copyright © 2012 by Stephen M. Kahnert

All rights reserved. No part of this book may be reproduced or transmitted in any form by any means whether graphic, electronic, or mechanical, including photocopying, recording, taping or by any information storage or retrieval system—except for brief quotations in printed or electronic reviews—without prior written permission from the publisher.

Although every precaution has been taken in preparation of this book, there may be errors, both typographical and in content. The publisher and author assume no responsibility for any errors or omissions. Neither is any liability assumed for damages resulting, directly or indirectly, from the use of the information contained herein.

Author: Stephen M. Kahnert

ISBN-10: 1480238554
ISBN-13: 978-1480238558

LCCN: 2012921441
Library of Congress subject headings:
1. Gratitude.
2. Generosity - Social aspects.
3. Philanthropy.
4. Corporations - Charitable contributions.

Publisher:
Stephen M. Kahnert
Des Plaines, Illinois
www.generosity-GENROZT.com

Cover illustration: Mony Bunni
Cover & interior design: Dave Vineis
First Reader: Peter M. M. Kahnert

First Printing
Printed in the United States of America

FOR MOM AND DAD

"Boys, the best gift we ever gave you was one another."

Christmas 2009

to honor Harvey's dictum!

Stephen

July 2024

ACKNOWLEDGEMENTS

Just as a tuning fork has two tines, gratitude paired with generosity resonates most wonderfully.

I am grateful to the hundreds of people who welcomed my author's quest from the scholars of Our Lady of Destiny Catholic School to my four friends of Chapter 11; from Tim Patterson to Joanie (Ralph) Muench; from Lt. Col. Steven Simon of the United States Air Force Academy to Bob Pierce of the University of Southern Mississippi; from Alice Hayes to Dave Hilliard.

Two notable subsets are my seven brothers, my four sons and my wife, Sheila Cawley, and the dozens named who are no longer with us on this side of reality but remain a vibrant part of it nonetheless.

I celebrate folks whose names don't appear but whose participation was critical: the community of my sons' school especially the ever-enthused Gina Rothweiler. My five Stein nephews with the gift of that pen and my former colleague, Becky Moore, for the gift of her friendship. And farther from home Linda Wicks, archivist for the Sisters of St. Joseph, and John Kastner, the editor of Stratford's *Beacon Herald* who actually let me leave his building to copy original Festival documents.

I am thankful for those who helped me get publishing things done like my local Alphagraphics and Walgreen's camera specialists even to asking, monthly, "How's your book coming?" My cover artist Mony Bunni and e-book publishing expert Lorraine Phillips, Stephanie Ferguson's friend. My proofreader Kathleen H. Sison and cover design-layout-website guy Dave Vineis.

I am indebted to my First Reader, Peter M.M. Kahnert, who – in our sunny back porch last July – skillfully called for the storyteller in me to outshine the journalist. To the degree the former succeeded, the latter wants Peter's guidance lauded.

Finally, I toast Charlie Brown's friend, Sparky, and Gregory Clark, described by Ernest Hemingway as "the best writer on the paper" when they both wrote for the *Toronto Star* in the 1920s. He was right.

Stephen M. Kahnert
Des Plaines, Illinois
Thanksgiving 2012

TABLE OF CONTENTS

Foreword by Dr. Alice B. Hayes, President (ret.)
University of San Diego

Introduction: As We Begin ...

Afterword by Dave Hilliard, President and CEO
Wyman Center in St. Louis and The Wyman National Network

About the Author

FOREWORD

Dr. Alice B. Hayes, President (ret.)
University of San Diego

A city becomes a community when it can offer such amenities as a library, a school, a park, a church, an art museum, a hospital, and perhaps a parade or two. Although some of these may have been built with tax revenues, most of these assets are provided to the community as gifts – some from the wealth of great philanthropists, others from the profits of a local corporation.

This book tells other stories, though, stories about people who changed lives in very quiet, unpretentious ways. There's a laundress, a railroad employee, and a beloved Latin teacher among often-unsung heroes. You might not know their names, but you will recognize their spirit of generosity that inspired this book.

There is nothing ordinary about the ordinary people in these tales. The author, Stephen Kahnert, has captured that with surprisingly rounded views of his subjects, presenting them with the warmth of personal friendship. Many of the conversations that form the heart of each chapter were conducted by Stephen in the company of his sons, a legacy of sensitive listening and articulate reflection that will surely shape their lives.

As someone who was pleased and privileged

to work with generous people, I am always amazed by the ready response to a community's needs by people with great hearts. People like these do not contribute because they need a tax deduction or want to see their names on buildings and in lights. They do not give because others have pressured them. Quite the opposite!

As Stephen's thoughtful essays reveal, generous people have particular character traits. They show remarkable persistence in addressing their concerns. Like the Stratford Festival's Tom Patterson, they cannot be dissuaded by discouraging words. Like Capt. Dale Noyd, they maintain their views even recognizing there might be negative consequences. When they take up a cause, it shapes their lives. They have achieved the goal set by Saint Ignatius "to give and not to mind the cost."

Generous people give exceptional attention and personal interest. Like hockey star Gordie Howe giving time to a little boy, or Gladys Holm in her wheelchair visiting hospitalized children with bins of teddy bears. Their outreach is not delegated to a secretary or a lawyer. It is personal, and comes directly from their own great spirits.

This is a book that will provide valuable insights for those seeking to understand the motivations and methods of those who contribute to their causes. I expect this book will be found on the desks of fundraisers and public relations officers, college presidents, and their many volunteer leaders. In these pages they will find their supporters, alumni, neighbors and friends.

But I suspect GENROZT will have an even wider audience: those of us who want to understand better the human heart and the influence of personal commitments on the growth of communities.

There is a contagious quality to the goodness of the people in these chapters. Those who know them come to not only admire them, but to emulate them. My hope is that this book will inspire others to have the courage to express their generous selves.

To keep our communities growing and serving, we need many more people like those profiled here. As Mother Teresa reminded us, "if we want to keep our lamps burning, we have to keep putting in oil." The generous people found in this book show us how to bring light to those around us.

Chicago, Illinois
September 2012

INTRODUCTION:
AS WE BEGIN...

The story of how my parents got son #8 is as good a place as any for me to start these memories of generosities.

I am the second oldest of seven sons born to Rita (Daly) and Bill Kahnert. Mom had five brothers and five sisters and she often told us of the conversation about family size Dad and she had after their April 1945 wedding at Our Lady of Perpetual Help in Toronto. Dad had one brother. "Well, average size," said Rita.

And so they had seven sons born to them – Thomas, Stephen, Patrick, Vincent, Peter, John, and Joseph. Along the way, friends would come through our back hall strewn with hockey sticks and coats ("Can't you boys straighten out this mess!!") and down to our basement to listen to music, to tell tales, and to chat with Mom in her laundry room. Rita was a terrific listener of guys.

And Bill listened to Rita's heart, which is how we got Mike, brother #8, who had been one of Vince's best friends since kindergarten. (Every family has a VinceNation – the one who stays in touch with dozens of friends as the years roll by.) Mike tells the story of how Rita appeared at his home the day of his Dad's funeral (his Mom had died young a few years before) and hugged him saying: "Well, Mike, now you belong to us."

Rita's simple, elegant declaration is at the core of this book on diverse generosities ... some I witnessed, some I lived, some I came across, usually through intriguing obituaries which, yes, Mom encouraged me to read! Along my path I've worked in fundraising for three decades, volunteered as a hockey coach and 1st grade Cool Reader, and been blessed with singular people like my wife, Sheila, my four sons, Matthew, Peter, Emmett and Liam, and my seven brothers.

My chapters have subtitles describing the generosities in each, and each is enriched by the memories of young scholars from Emmett and Liam's grade school, Our Lady of Destiny in Des Plaines, Illinois, class of 2011-2012. (I told them they'd recognize generosity by thinking about people with good hearts.) My final chapter presents the memories of four friends who responded to my request to remember, and then write up, their special generosity memory.

At long last I've arrived at a definition of GENROZT, the word that greets me daily on my Illinois license plate: *a gracious act that creates a joyful ache every time it is remembered.* Like beauty, GENROZT is in the eye of the beholder.

As you read these chapters, think about your own GENROZT story and how you can enrich our world by telling it to someone. Soon.

The word that greets me daily.

1
TOM'S SECOND LETTER
generosities of heart, of listening, of words, of action

William Shakespeare helped get me my greatest summer job ever – editor of the weekly *Grand Bend Times*, the summer before my third year in Honours (sic) English Language & Literature at St. Michael's College. The summer of 1970 was also the 18th season of Tom Patterson's great creation, Stratford's Shakespearean Festival, just 90 miles west of our Toronto home.

You really should know about the man who got me that job. About the generosities that influenced his life. And his second letter to me. Let's begin with Tom's *New York Times* obituary:

"Mr. Patterson (June 11, 1920 – February 23, 2004) was a journalist with no theatrical credentials when he became smitten with the idea of casting the Bard of Stratford-on-Avon as the savior of Stratford, Ontario. A small town on the wane, it boasted its own River Avon, but was vanishing along with its earlier livelihood, servicing locomotives."

That poetic phrase "when he became smitten" led me to a key influence in Tom's life, Miss Rose McQueen, his English teacher at Stratford Collegiate Institute.

The first time I met her was on page 163 of Tom's book *They Never Rationed Courage*, a collection of his WWII letters home. There in a lengthy February 1943 note to his Mom, Lucinda, a thoughtful 23-year-old wrote:

"I think the three things for my education that I can be thankful for are my home, the Stamps [the English couple that befriended him], and Rose McQueen. If I can't make a success of my life after all those blessings ..."

So, the summer of 2010 – forty years after my adventure as newspaper editor-photographer-delivery boy in a Lake Huron resort town – I drove from Chicago to Stratford with Peter, my rising college freshman, to learn more about Tom's Rose, and the role she played in his gift to me.

I had written to then-general manager of the Stratford Festival, Antoni Cimolino, and by email I was introduced to Wilfrid Gregory, an elderly former Festival Board leader. On a hot July morning I left Peter asleep in our motel room overlooking corn and drove the few blocks to Wilf's home near the Avon River.

A motorized wheelchair was Wilf's only nod to his 98 years and, after our light breakfast, he zipped over to many Festival-related folders laid out for me. Wilf ("I was named for Prime Minister Laurier") had a full career as a lawyer, business leader, community builder, and fourth Chairman of the Shakespearean Festival Board in 1960. He smiled often as we chatted.

Wilf handed me his eulogy on Tom, delivered from the stage of the Festival Theatre, starting with how a young associate editor of a trade magazine button-holed Stratford's mayor in May 1951. Tom thought that a city with wards named Hamlet, Falstaff, Romeo, Shakespeare, and Avon should try something big.

"Tom underplayed his persistent attitude by encouraging people to help him with his plans," Wilf wrote, "but his goals were pre-established and non-negotiable: he was absolutely certain that he would have a Festival ...

"Stratford's new Festival Committee agreed with Tom's proposal that he should go to New York to talk to Sir Laurence Olivier. Tom ... hoped that he might ask him for advice on his project. Tom asked the City of Stratford for a grant of $100 for his expenses for the trip.

"This request came to me as chairman of the Industrial and Publicity Committee and it passed unanimously, except that we raised the amount to $125 (I had been to a meeting in Toronto the week before at a cost of $82.50 and knew that $100 was not enough.) That $125 seems very small these days, but it was sufficient then.

"As it turned out, Tom could not get to see Sir Laurence because he was out of town, but Tom was smart enough to use some of his time in New York to visit two eminent foundations [which] resulted in a Rockefeller grant two years later." And then Wilf described how Tom's passion prevailed.

"Tom gave up his magazine job and took on the management of the Festival with no money even to pay him for his expenses, let alone finance the tremendous job of producing a program for 1953 ... in the end, everything came together on time and on budget. It was a success.

"It was also a miracle! That process is not recommended as a business plan for a budding entrepreneur – except one with the vision and determination and personality of Tom Patterson. Tom was unique."

Before leaving, I learned that Wilf graduated high school in 1929, 10 years before Tom, and they shared the same English teacher, a core influence on all her students. Miss McQueen had the ability to control a class by capturing the interest and respect of students. She was on the stout side, he recalled, pleasant-looking, stern. She was a great teacher. She always said, "let's put on Shakespeare plays here!"

Later that day, I met with Kate Jacob of the Stratford-Perth Archives to learn more about Tom's self-described "blessing", Rose McQueen.

Among documents by and about Rose, Kate found newspaper clippings, her October 1963 obituary, and Stratford Collegiate yearbooks (there's Tom in the 1937 "Collegian" as yearbook staff and manager of the Junior hockey team. Justin Bieber

Wilf and me in his Stratford living room, sporting our Will Power! pins

probably passed photos of Tom in their high school hallways.)

In 1985 another of Miss McQueen's students, Ernest Stabler, a retired Dean at the University of Western Ontario, wrote that "[she] brought to her classes a presence and a sense of dignity and grace, warmth and humour of a subtle kind, and an abiding love for the English word."

He quoted another former student:

"Much has been hinted that [Rose] had a great influence on Tom Patterson, and indeed she had. In my heart I feel that after Tom had got the Festival off the ground, some of its success was the result of enthusiasm in the hearts and minds of her former students. She lit the flame that started the Festival, and her spirit kept the fire going through the years."

Before heading home, I stopped at Miss McQueen's home of many years on Waterloo Street. You can almost see the theatre named for her student, Tom, from her front door.

I left Stratford enthused about the generosities that touched Tom's life: Rose McQueen's love of words; town leaders' support; the partnership of directors and actors; and gifts like the anonymous one in 1953 when the need was greatest from Canada's Governor-General, Vincent Massey, actor Raymond's brother.

Armed with these insights, I wrote to one of Tom's sons and on a bright Saturday in September 2011, Tim and his wife Aileen welcomed me to their Toronto-area home.

All smiles, Tim began with a tour of many walls covered with Tom's photos and clippings and awards ending in their living room next to a bust of his dad. It was wearing a captain's hat.

Over Earl Grey tea, I learned that Tim was born on June 16, 1953, less than a month to the opening of that first Festival season; that the future Captain Kirk, William Shatner, attended his baptism; that his 5' 4½" Dad always sported a bowtie; that Tom once suggested that U.S. and Russian leaders defrost the Cold War by watching Festival plays; and that his dad was a great listener who would talk with anyone "whether you were royalty or the guy in the parking lot."

Big ideas weren't confined to Tom in the Patterson home. His first wife, Tim's mother Robin, for many years headed the Canadian Players organization created in 1954 to help Stratford actors earn off-season money by bringing Shakespeare to "the highways and byways of Canada." When she first met Tom seven years earlier he had told her of his Festival dream and Robin "encouraged his dreaming and planning."

Tim told me that his Aunt Florence – still alive and kicking – took a leap of faith and left her job to become the Festival's first full-time employee. When I later spoke with her by phone, Aunt Florence recalled, "no one seemed very generous in the beginning ... there were many rejections, including a man who wrote, 'we don't want strangers walking across our grass' in the local paper."

Standing in the sunshine as they walked me to my car, Aileen mentioned "a recent *Globe and Mail* editorial that wondered 'what if Tom Patterson hadn't gotten his $125!'" and Tim summarized his dad as "an unassumingly generous man."

Which brings us to the day I wrote to Tom Patterson asking for a summer job.

As I remember it, in November 1969 I read an article about the Stratford Festival in my mom's newest *Reader's Digest*. I was determined to work with the guy who boldly called the world's leading Shakespearean director, Tyrone Guthrie, at his home in Ireland asking him to come and help start a Festival!

So, in youthful confidence I sat down at my old manual Remington typewriter and asked. As winter ended I was puzzled at no reply and worried that summer 1970 would see me cutting grass and painting houses.

Then a letter arrived with the return address 140 Norman Street, Stratford, dated April 6, my mother Rita's 49th birthday. Tom apologized that my letter had been mislaid, that he had called the Festival on my behalf to no avail, and then suggested some Stratford contacts I could try, finishing up with:

"I am sorry I cannot be of more help and again ask humble apologies for not responding immediately to your bright and cheerful letter ..."

To say I was crushed is an understatement (those were my green, youthful days when I assumed every initiative I tried would be successful!). And then, most wondrously, another envelope from Tom arrived the very next day, sent so quickly the six-cent stamp with a dark-haired Queen Elizabeth wasn't even canceled. I still have it.

Tom's second letter was also dated April 6:

"This is really a P.S. to my other letter. On the

way to the Post Office I ran into the manager of the *Stratford Times* who asked: 'You don't know anybody I could get to take over as editor of our *Grand Bend Times* paper?' I told him I had just posted a letter to you and I thought you might possibly be the right man for him."

But, best of all – most generously of all – Tom's last paragraph, just above his creative, enthusiastic signature is the poem he wrote. To me.

"As Shakespeare would say

> *From here on'st*
> *The torch I passeth over*
> *With great hopes*
> *That the Times shall forthwith*
> *Enhance their reputation and your pocket*
> *From the use of delicate words"*

Holding that letter, if you were a 20 year-old English major, and the author-poet was the accomplished 50 year-old founder of the Stratford Shakespearean Festival, how would you have felt?

That's exactly how I felt too.

As editor of the *Grand Bend Times* – sandy beaches, roller rink, and Credence Clearwater Revival hits an easy drive from Detroit – I worked my territory in shorts and t-shirts from late June through Labor Day. Just like you would've done, I've kept copies.

It was 25 years later that I finally met Tom face to face when visiting family in Toronto. He agreed to see me though he had undergone surgery and spoke through a hole in his throat. Tom – alert and ever-gracious – and his wife, Pat, welcomed me to their garden apartment.

Soon after that "smitten" reference in Tom's *New York Times* obituary we read:

"What Mr. Patterson lacked in knowledge about staging plays, he more than made up with sheer persistence...Conceived as a national venture [the Festival] attracted a first-rate acting company starting with its first year... . The recipient of many awards, [Tom] made an emotional appearance before a capacity audience for 'Richard III' at the festival's 50th season in 2002 ..."

Director Tyrone Guthrie is quoted in *Renown at Stratford*: "He had no great influence to back him, no great reputation, no great fortune. Most of us similarly placed abandon our Great Ideas, wrote them off as Daydreams, and settled for something less exciting and more practicable. Not so Mr. Patterson. His perseverance was indomitable."

Will's *Troilus and Cressida* described that virtue when he had Ulysses affirm to Achilles: "Perseverance, my lord, keeps honour bright."

I never recall my generous, tenacious friend without a joyful ache. Every time.

GENROZT

I think my cousin Sophia has a big heart because she is funny. She is all ways happy. She is all ways nice. She likes me a lot. and loves me too.

Denise F. 1st grade

When I was in class we had to write Social Studies definitions. I hadn't finished all of the definitions yet, and I was running out of time. I just needed to finish and I would have no homework. My friends were done and they helped me finish the definitions, and we all ended up having no homework at all.

Samantha B. 4th grade

My favorite generosity memory was at a Chicago Cubs game 2 years ago. The man behind my family accidentally spilled his entire beer on my brother. He felt so bad he offered to buy my brother anything he wanted from the concession stand. At another Cubs game when I was 8 I waited for the players to come out for an autograph but they didn't. This guy saw I was sad and gave me a Cubs hat signed by Michael Barrett. He literally took it off his head and put it on mine.

Max R. 7th grade

"All money is congealed energy."

Joseph Campbell to Bill Moyers in *The Power of Myth*, edited by
Betty Sue Flowers who thanked Jacqueline Kennedy Onassis
"whose interest in the ideas of Joseph Campbell was the prime
mover in the publication of this book."

2

JOAN EVELYN'S PATH
generosities of heart, of listening, of effort, of vision

It's not often a middle-aged white guy falls in love with a 72-year old black grandmother. I'm the white guy; she is Joan Evelyn Southgate.

Our short story is this: On a sunny spring afternoon in 2002, son #2 Peter and I met up with the singular Joan Evelyn on her 519-mile walk – 10 miles per day, sleeping in strangers' homes – following the Underground Railroad (URR) path from Kentucky to Canada with her mission to change our world.

But it's the long version you'll want to hear.

On Wednesday, February 26, 1997, I became a naturalized U.S. citizen with son #1 Matthew at my side. Before leaving the courthouse I joined the League of Women Voters because voting has always been a key measure of citizenship for me. I accepted that my Canadian birth couldn't be an excuse for ignorance about American realities and I knew that learning racism was way different than learning baseball.

So I began.

And I'm sharing this with you because it's critical to my finding Joan Evelyn.

In my new-citizen file, I still have the January 2000 newspaper story about a photography exhibit of American lynchings between 1883 and 1960. The photo with the article shows maybe three dozen faces of white men and boys, some smiling into the camera, while a black youth hangs from the tree branch above their heads. Such photos were even made into postcards for spectators to mail.

Here's a March 2002 article from Cleveland's *The Plain Dealer* about visiting high school basketball players and fans taunting their Oberlin rivals with everything including the 'n' word. In Oberlin of all places, an historic anti-slavery community, a wellspring of tolerance where URR stop #99 still stands!

I had just seen ESPN's story of Frederick Douglass "Fritz" Pollard, who grew up in Chicago, graduated from Brown University, was the first black to play in the Rose Bowl, the first black quarterback in pro football, and who went on to be a leading entertainment agent during the Harlem Renaissance of the 1920s.

The piece ends with Fritz on his couch, erect and sharp at 92, tears in his eyes, still remembering those cruel college football fans singing "Bye Bye Blackbird" as he took the field.

So I contacted ESPN and, through the generosity of their production team, I was sent a copy of his story to share with those Oberlin-area high schools. Within days of receiving that video, I read about a diminutive grandmother's URR path north through Oberlin then east to St. Catharines, Ontario, Canada.

You should know that I tend to be bold.

So, I left a voicemail for Margaret Bernstein of *The Plain Dealer* asking if she'd hook us up to Joan on her walk. Which is how Peter and I – returning from his 4th grade history trip to Cincinnati – were standing in a room at Antioch College in Yellow Springs, Ohio, waiting for Joan that bright spring day in 2002.

She had already walked her 10 miles that morning and afterward, as planned, met with school students and made new friends talking about – and listening to – stories of hope and courage and freedom. She did this every day.

Joan Evelyn Southgate walked into that hot, sunny room and, beaming, walked right by me to talk to nine-year-old Peter. That's when I knew.

She chatted with him about his schoolwork and his project on President Wm. Howard Taft, in no rush to turn toward any others in the room, also waiting for her voice. This is what she wrote on the top of the article about her that Peter was carrying: Thank you for coming to Yellow Springs. I repeat as I walk – "whatever you can do, or dream you can, begin it. Boldness has power, and magic in it."

In driving north to our Cleveland-area home, we hatched plans for Joan to stay in "safe houses," with Peter's school friends and with us too. And, feeding that back to Joan, we asked if she would stop and speak at Peter's elementary school in almost-all-white Bay Village.

When Joan walked into Peter's school's gym, she was greeted by 200 smiling 4th graders and later, after her presentation, the school buses were delayed as dozens of students stood in line to get Joan's autograph on the photo of her that each of them was wearing that day.

Joan had rock-star impact in that gym, gracious and open, heartfelt and generous. And Peter chose the photo of him with Joan for his "Now I'm 10" frame that May. He's wearing a t-shirt commemorating 9/11, which hit in his first weeks of 4th grade in Mrs. Appell's class.

Joan Evelyn and Peter at the end of the first leg of her URR walk, Peter still wearing Joan's picture

Soon after finishing her walk, Joan wrote *In Their Path*, a memoir about her journey. You've got to get your own copy and mark it up as I have done. My underlines include Joan's degrees (*cum laude* from Syracuse University in 1952; MSW from Cleveland's Western Reserve University in 1954); her careers as an activist and social worker; and her encounter with little Helen on page 136, the day she met my Peter:

"At another Yellow Springs school, Mills Lawn School, I had talked about slaves deciding to run to freedom and asked the roomful of 7- to 1-year-olds to think about how they must have felt. What would a family plan? What would you take with you? ... Then one small, blond child sitting cross-legged on the floor in the front row raised her hand to quietly answer: 'They would have to take their hope with them.'

"I was stunned. I could hardly believe my ears. 'What did you say?'

'They would have to take their hope with them.'

If, as I think will happen, you too are swept up by Joan Evelyn, you'll find copies of her other books and meet her extended Harris famly, particularly her mother, Evelyn. And you too you will ache in the quiet of her "Nelson Mandela" reflection and rejoice in "To the Meadows" which begins, "Something Mother sang into my soul prescribed a passion to make me tough and joyous."

On the day Joan "stepped off," as she called it, on the final URR leg from Cleveland east to Canada, she departed from the rickety steps of a decrepit home on Mayfield Road, the last Civil War-era home with URR connections.

The Cozad family and their neighbors, the Fords, owned much of the land now called University Circle, where Case Western Reserve University, the Cleveland Museum of Art, the Botanical Garden, the Natural History Museum, and the Cleveland Orchestra's Severance Hall comprise much of the city's cultural heart.

When Joan started east, the house was owned by University Hospitals, one of the region's largest healthcare providers. It was in a sorry state, shakily protected from demolition by its 1974 National Register of Historic Places status. Since then, many generous caretakers had watched over that house, most especially Mrs. Nesbitt, who lived in the apartment across the street. On her walks across two decades, she would circle that house daily on her "guardian angel" strolls.

Before her trek, Joan had no idea that the URR name for the Cleveland station was *Hope*. Within days of returning from Canada, she gathered six women at her dining room table to create a plan to save the Cozad-Bates house.

Joan's home is east of downtown Cleveland,

just off Martin Luther King Drive which runs through a shallow valley strewn with trees from Lake Erie to University Circle. That drive is one of Cleveland's best assets, and the dozens of cultural gardens strung along the eastern ridge are stunning, if little known. (The fellow who promoted those gardens, Charles Wolfram, always spoke of brotherhood as the goal of the gardens.)

When you walk up the wooden stairs to Joan's bright blue home, and on through to her dining room you will read what those six women read, because the words are still on her wall a decade later. High up (which is sweet since Joan is barely five feet tall) running along three of the four walls, on butcher paper is this:

May I be filled with loving kindness. May I be well. May I be peaceful and at ease, may I be joyful!

And Joan Evelyn Southgate is.

She found that quote in a book by Jack Kornfield. She's never taken it down because she isn't finished yet. Just underneath, among the newspaper clippings and photos on her walls, you will read the words of Goethe that accompanied her every step along those 519 miles, the ones she wrote on Peter's newspaper, the ones that are still with her.

The plans those ladies started at Joan's table became *Restore Cleveland Hope*. One of the group's first efforts was a candlelight vigil in front of the

Cozad-Bates house, led by the smiling, magnetic Joan. Sheila, one-year-old son #3, Emmett, and I were among the 50 intrepid souls in the rain that October evening, and the next day's paper quoted Joan on the goal of *Restore Cleveland Hope*: "We will turn this house into a safe house, safe for creativity and collaboration."

Understandably, the spokeswoman for University Hospitals was reticent, quoting restoration estimates of $2 million. Soon after, diverse leaders created a plan to transfer ownership of the house from the hospital to a local nonprofit and start the long process of restoration.

But Joan isn't done.

Restore Cleveland Hope initiatives and a rehabilitated Civil War-era house are just vessels. What Joan really wants is a beloved community for us, the beloved community Rev. Martin Luther King, Jr., described as built on the three pillars of Reconciliation, Freedom, and Hope.

Because talk is cheap, Joan Evelyn listens more than she talks. She is serious about this beloved community in our midst, investing her days practicing more reconciliation, more freedom, more hope enticing people like you and me into her quest, one by one.

This past summer Peter (now a rising junior at The Ohio State University) and I rolled up to Joan's house with Emmett and son #4, Liam. After a meal overseen by those dining room quotes, we strolled through the cultural gardens, up the hills Joan used to train for her walk, and then back to her kitchen table.

"What I still can't quite grasp is that ten years later something is still happening," Joan began. "I thought I was on a journey that had a beginning and an end … but it never stopped!" One of her fondest memories of a decade back is being greeted by that gym filled with children each wearing her photo. And there at Joan's kitchen table Peter, now six foot three, just smiled and smiled.

Another activist whose journey never stopped was Studs Terkel, Chicago's raconteur, writer, broadcaster, and goad who would have been 100 on May 16, 2012. A few hundred of us gathered to mark his life at a place Studs loved, The Newberry Library, where many speakers used the word "generosity" toasting him.

Studs – who, like Joan, was on the short side – would talk with and listen to regular folks, then write up their insights. "What I do is try to celebrate the lives of the uncelebrated," he would explain.

Ten years before Joan Evelyn's journey, Studs wrote his book *How Blacks and Whites Think and Feel About the American Obsession* telling an interviewer, "You overcome racism by knowing what the other person's life was like…. Listen to the other person."

Tough and joyous indeed.

GENROZT

When I was three I was playing on a scooter and tipped over and fell onto a barbeque. I burned my arm. Dr. Quigley helped me. She gave me good moisture and a bandage and a stuffed buffalo that I named Quigley.

Liam K. kindergarten

My classmate Auggie helped me with German homework. Auggie could've been playing something else with his friends. Auggie is very generous. He spent so much time helping me.

Jane R. 3rd grade

One time I was over at my Nana and Papa's house. They always say to be caring and kind to everyone you meet. This time was different. It was different because my Nana told me that you should never regret anything you do in life and to never give up. And to this day I always remember her telling me that! It was one of the greatest moments.

Angela B. 8th grade

3

GORDIE'S HUG
generosities of heart, of coaching, of time

There are many examples of great hearts in my first-floor room dedicated to all things hockey. It's just off the living room and holds Sheila's piano, our elliptical exercise machine (hey, I could be called up any day now) and 102 posters, photos, drawings, action figures, tabletop hockey game, and a six-foot Abraham Lincoln in goalie equipment. More on him later.

They all warm me and some bring tears to my eyes. But the one that I cherish most is the photo of my eldest son, then-seven-year-old Matthew, in his hockey sweater next to a smiling, well-dressed grandfather, Gordie Howe.

To appreciate the lasting impact of Gordie's hug, you should know about the company he keeps on the walls of my hockey grotto.

To Gordie's right is the black and white photo of the 1972-73 St. Gabriel pee wee team. That was the year Vince, brother #4, and I coached John, brother #6, all the way to the championship game. (Dad would always introduce us by birth order: Tom #1, me #2, Pat #3, Vince #4, Peter #5, John #6, Joseph #7. Some say #7 was our best hockey player; others say #6; Pat says #3 was.)

A referee's bad call caused the league to reschedule the final few minutes of the big game, starting with John taking a penalty shot that could tie it up, and send it into overtime. Etched on my heart is the warm, gracious generosity of Mrs. McCann, the mother of John's best friend, Mike, the captain of the other team. The memory of her standing by the boards as John took the ice, wishing him luck, always brings me to tears. It transcends John's shot to this day.

Just to Gordie's left is a photo of four players, two dads and two sons, kneeling on a frozen pond. I wish for you the timely generosity of a co-coach like Bob Shaffalo, and a photo on your wall that reminds you.

Just beyond that photo, hanging beneath the poster of vintage Zamboni ice machines, is a reflection on the life of John Rogers, a beloved Toronto neighbor and avid Detroit Red Wings fan. It is by his son Gord and granddaughter Sarah with the subtitle "Hockey fan, family man, teller of tales."

Every year he would make an outdoor rink in his small backyard at 16 Caracas Road for his nine kids, inevitably joined by us seven from 26, and the five McGouran boys at 17.

Our Mr. Rogers coached hockey for decades, specializing in beginners—Vince was the first of us he inherited. One even got into the NHL. And everyone he coached skated on in life, buoyed by

John's generous spirit.

Standing on Sheila's piano is a coffee mug — well, almost a chalice—from Gordie Howe's Tavern & Eatery in Traverse City which a buddy, who loves the Boston Bruins, found for me.

Now, let me explain about that six-foot Abraham Lincoln.

A few years ago, I got to wondering what position Lincoln would have played if he had played hockey. Then I wrote it up, and got my then-14-year-old nephew Matthew Stein to draw him as a goalie in the pose all hockey aficionados know as the one favored by Ken Dryden of the Montreal Canadiens.

Months after mailing our poster to scads of hockey and Lincoln-related groups, a letter arrived from the Abraham Lincoln Presidential Library & Museum in Springfield, Illinois. It was a gracious message from the chief of the Lincoln Collection, James Cornelius, with the news that it was now in the collection. (Curator James played hockey as a youngster. He wore Bobby Orr's #4.)

All very cool.

Which brings me to Gordie's hug.

Until that October Sunday, I had never asked celebrities, sports stars or corporate titans I met for their autographs. "Oh sure," you might think. "That's sour grapes. He's never gotten close enough to ask!" Not true. In my nonprofit and corporate work I have shaken hands with the usual suspects among politicians, athletes, and entertainers. I admired them all. No autographs. No pix.

Until 1994 – the year I turned 45 (the same age Gordie was when he came out of retirement to join the World Hockey Association's Houston Aeros); until seven months after Wayne Gretzky passed Gordie Howe's NHL total goals record; until a few minutes after 6 a.m. Sunday, October 23, 1994, to be exact.

That fall weekend #9 of the Detroit Red Wings was slated to drop the ceremonial puck at the first hockey game in my adopted hometown with the visiting Detroit Vipers taking on the Cleveland Lumberjacks. Before that Sunday, I had three Gordie imprints on my hockey soul:

1. wearing my Red Wings sweater, #9, when I was Matthew's age

2. attending the last game Gordie played in one of hockey's temples, Toronto's Maple Leaf Gardens

3. working with a client in the snows of Saskatoon, Saskatchewan — Gordie's territory where hockey cards are heirlooms

Only a face-to-face chat was lacking. Gordie, Matthew and me.

Gordie Imprint #1

I know, I know, I should have given up sucking my fingers long before my seventh birthday. But sleeping in one bedroom with four brothers generated understandable stress, with two more rookies yet to join us.

Anyway, Uncle Pat, mom's traveling salesman brother, would often stay with us overnight on the chesterfield in the living room. Stubbing out his cigarette, he cut me this deal: "Stephen, if you stop sucking your fingers by my next trip, I will buy you a hockey outfit of your own."

I did. He did. And that winter I was landing on the ice after jumping the snow fence at the end of our yard, resplendent in my Detroit Red Wings uniform, sweater #9. The only one of us brothers who shot right, just like Gordie.

Gordie Imprint #2

We used to harangue Mom to buy Sheriff's Jello though most of us didn't eat it for dessert. In those days every box came with a hockey coin of a player on one of the original six NHL teams. You really should know their names. Like Inca gold they were. We played road hockey games that carried over to the next day when night fell, to the next brother when a new one arrived. In our home, the theme music to *Hockey Night in Canada* was like a second national anthem.

So the chance to see Gordie play his final NHL game in Toronto was worth every hockey coin, every hockey memory, my family ever possessed.

John Gerard Olaf – as Dad loved calling him – had a buddy whose family had first-class season tickets to Leafs games. "Go ahead. My dad's away and won't be using them" we were told. So we settled into terrific seats, blithely unaware that his dad was flying home early for that historic game.

John and I spent three periods marveling at why no one seemed able to hit #9 in New England Whalers' green (his dexterity at age 52? their reverence? his rising elbows?). We made no attempt at an autograph. It was enough to be in Gordie's presence along with 16,000 other fans that spring evening of 1980.

Gordie Imprint #3

In early 1994, I was working with an economic-development client in Saskatoon's minus-30 degree Celsius weather. Look that up; that's wickedly frigid. Airport rental cars came with 30-foot extension cords for plugging the engine block into electrical outlets on parking posts.

A bronze statue of Gordie had been unveiled (elbows up, his back to the Toys R Us store) so I bought a disposable camera for a few keepsake shots. Captured in another rush up-ice, Gordie's eyes are looking left, waiting for the pass from #7

Ted Lindsay. That winter Wayne Gretzky #99 finally passed #9's NHL goals record of 801 and went on to set new, astounding records. Big time.

Wayne breaking Gordie's record was captured by many artists, including Mike Graston of *The Windsor Star*. His editorial cartoon shows a little player leaving a hockey rink holding his dad's hand, the latter saying "Just because of what Gretzky's done, as a longtime fan of Gordie Howe I resent being called a fossil!"

"Just like Matthew and me," I thought! And I bought it. For Matthew, of course.

These Gordie imprints inspired me the second-last weekend of October in the Year of Our Lord One Thousand, Nine Hundred, and Ninety-Four.

So I called the head of the Lumberjack's marketing group, a former goaltender who regularly coached the St. Edward's Eagles to state high school championships. "Bob," I asked, "how can I get 10 minutes alone with Gordie for my son Matthew?"

And he said, "Where will you be at 6 a.m. the morning after the game?" Which is equivalent to oversleeping in the hockey world. "Anywhere you tell me to be."

Then he made me a generous offer. "Gordie has to catch an early Northwest flight back to Detroit. Why don't you and your son pick him up at his hotel downtown and have 30 minutes with him as you drive to the airport?"

I've never met a Bob I didn't like.

Matthew went to bed in his light blue North Olmsted House League hockey sweater #9 that Saturday night. As we drove off to get Gordie in the morning darkness, I was remembering all the nights I slept in my sweater with Christmas-morning-like expectation, waiting to leave for our games with Tom #1 in front and Dad (O Captain, my Captain) at the wheel.

Gordie came into the Stouffer Hotel's lobby with a suitcase that must have been three feet square and a foot thick. "He will act exactly like your grandfather," I told a wondering Matthew. And he did. Warm, outgoing, thoughtful, and humorous at 6:15 a.m.

My Gordie and my Matthew

We three were joined in our minivan by Bob Ufer, President of the International Hockey League, who was in for the first game too. He graciously sat beside Matthew in the bench seat, behind Gordie and me.

The conversation in our drive west touched on NHL Oldtimers games, on a new Gordie Howe clothing line about to preview, and on Gordie's family. And I'm pretty sure talk of my Saskatoon adventures marked me as A True Adherent.

Too soon the trip to the airport was over, the sun still unseen. Gordie was in no hurry to leave us, laconically finishing a story that graciously wrapped me into his audience. The moment Matthew and I planned had arrived. "Gordie, we were wondering if you might sign a few things for us?" Sure, he says.

Bob leans forward to read the editorial cartoon I handed across and they both chuckle as Gordie signs 'Gordon,' not Gordie, Howe. Looking over his shoulder at Matthew, he turns back to sign a picture of his statue "To Matthew – see you in the NHL."

It's not yet 7 a.m. on a dark, chilly Sunday morning and my hockey hero is remembering my half-asleep seven-year-old Mite in the back seat. Go ahead. Tell me that happens every time you meet a professional athlete.

Since Gordie still wasn't moving to open his door, I produced a photo that brother #3 (not named for Uncle Pat, he swears!) found for me, the only Detroit Red Wings fan among his brothers.

It's a Detroit vs. Toronto game, maybe 1965. Howe is cutting from left to right in front of the Leafs net with Johnny Bower at the top of his crease, hand sliding up his goalie stick about to try his patented poke check. Alex Delvecchio #10, Alan Stanley #26, and Eddie Shack #22 are in the background.

The puck is near Gordie's right skate, his head is down in that eternal second prior to a scintillating goal or a brilliant stop. "Gordie, Matthew and I have been studying this photo and it looks like Bower will poke check you. What do you think?"

He looks it over carefully. "Well look how my left skate is protecting the puck," says Gordie. "That's a goal!"

Years later in his autobiography *Gordie Howe, My Hockey Memories*, he recounted a routine he and his fishing buddy Bower had: "I always say 'Hey, John, I remember that play – I scored that goal,' and he always replies, 'Gordie, I don't think you ever scored on me, but this play I remember you shot wide.'"

Gordie happily agrees to a photo with Matthew and, just before I took the shot, he gave my first-born a warm, generous hug to get him to laugh.

Among the 102 mementos in my first-floor room is a photo of Howe and Bower signed, "Scores again. Gordon Howe." It hangs next to the photo of a smiling, well-dressed grandfather and an elated boy in his light-blue hockey sweater.

Gordie's elbows are down.

GENROZT

I think Abby Y. has a big heart because she shares with me and she plays with me and she is also very nice. She shares her stuffed animals books and toys.

Isabella S. 1st grade

What is generosity to me? That is easy. My neighbor Mr. Harold. When I was 7 months old my father died. My Mom was always scared and was crying. But soon, my neighbor, Mr. Harold was there to help. But Mr. Harold is blind. He could still help my Mom though. He would do things like put salt on our sidewalk ice, shovel our driveway, come every day and just give my Mom a hug. It would make her smile. His wife would always make me lemon cookies to cheer me up. I hope Mr. Harold and his wife stay healthy and live long.

Nicole P. 5th grade

My favorite generosity memory would have to be during my Dad's heart attack. It was the Stanley Cup and the Chicago Blackhawks were in it and winning. In the newspaper there would be a section with a player from the Hawks in it. About every week somebody would give it to me. They didn't have to give it to me but they did ... I still have all of the posters hanging up on my wall right now.

Madeline B. 8th grade

4

JOEL'S HOUSE
generosities of heart, of home, of a dinner bell

Sometimes when Louise Ralph turns into her long driveway, she remembers a station wagon jammed with kids stuck in the blowing snow, maybe halfway to the large, white house. And she smiles.

When my friend Joanie heard about this book and my stories about simple, powerful generosities she told me I absolutely had to talk with her mom. Which is how Emmett, Liam and I visited Louise in Springfield, Illinois, last summer and learned how Joel's house chose the large Ralph family almost 40 winters ago.

Before we left, Joanie gave me some background info:

- She is one of nine Ralph children, the eldest of the six girls.
- On a limited budget, Louise and her husband, Bob, were looking – and praying – for a bigger home and yard for their family.
- A widower sold the Ralph family his 10-room house for about half of what he originally asked.

Over lemonade and fresh donuts, Louise recounted how Joel Eastham's house was found, and the impact Joel's gracious act – selling it for a song, really – continues to have. (FYI Louise is a slim, dynamic grandmother who is a wizard at PacMan. She clobbered Liam, six, a few times before we headed back to Chicago!)

The arrival of their ninth, Dennis, inspired Louise, a teacher, to check Homes For Sale ads and Bob, an accountant, to run the numbers. They owned a small house on the north side of Springfield next door to a tavern and across a busy street from the Illinois State Fairgrounds. The six girls slept in the large dormer at the top of the house and the three boys in a smaller dormer.

"We had to go through the boys' room to go downstairs to the bathroom," Joanie remembers. "There were those old-style heating vents on the floor and we'd lie on our pillows, listening to the goings-on downstairs. Especially my Dad's 40th birthday party! The thing I loved best about that house is we were all together."

Before we go on, there are the makings of a terrific movie here. One of those quirky, independent films that play at the Sundance Film Festival headed by Robert Redford. I'd ask him to play Joel. He'd like that.

To play Joanie's dad we'd need an actor that does quiet and resolute really well. A fabulous scene would be the day Bob Ralph came home to tell his then-only-six kids and Louise he'd just quit his job.

The firm he worked for demanded that he alter some accounting numbers. Bob refused. Soon after, he got a job with the city, thank goodness, but refused to let a Commissioner put his election sign on their front lawn, regularly taking it down. Totally Gregory Peck.

For Louise, I'd say after meeting her only once, we've got to get someone feisty and clever and singular. Katharine Hepburn would be perfect.

To keep our credits straight, the real names and ages of the nine Ralph siblings when they bought Joel's house are – in birth order – Bobby (13), Joanie (12), Angie (11), Molly (10), Stephen (8), Maureen (6), Susie (4), Rosie (3), and baby Dennis (2).

Joanie is a Doris Day-with-Attitude type. Pert, positive, perseverant.

Not having met the rest of Joanie's clan, but believing all the tales I've heard, her five sisters might be drawn from that *Little Women* movie, the 1949 version. (Should be minimal arguing over which Ralph sister Elizabeth Taylor portrays.) Those guys from *Ghostbusters* could play Joanie's three brothers. Yeah.

To play the realtors who brought the deal together how about Susan Sarandon as Fran, and Michael Douglas will play John "Scotty" McAuley, Fran's broker.

Then there are the Easthams. One of Joel's daughters, Susan, called to describe her dad ("he built all the furniture in our doll house; he adored Mom!"), her mom (high school English teacher; "always put others before herself") and sisters Muriel, Mary, and brother David. I figure Audrey Hepburn for Joel's wife, Muriel, and the cast of that BBC movie on the Bronte family to play their children.

That troupe would be the cat's pajamas, as they say.

Back to Louise and the scene with the snowbound car in the driveway of Joel's house. It was December 1973.

"We had been looking at houses for months by then," said Louise. "But we weren't finding anything in our $25,000 to $30,000 price range. So, I asked the kids to pray a 54-day novena with me asking for help to find our next house. But a few weeks later, my sister called to tell us her teenage daughter was diagnosed with leukemia. Of course we redirected all of our prayers for Lisa.

"Before Christmas we drove to a lovely neighborhood on the south side of the city to look at a used bike for Bobby. And there it was, on Chatham Road, a For Sale sign on a big yard in front of this big white house.

"When we got home, I called the realtor, Fran, to learn that the owner's wife had died and he was eager to sell. The house was starting its second winter on the market and the owner was about to drop the asking price. Fran was very keen to show it to us.

"I vividly remember how the kids ran through that wonderful house, picking out their bedrooms! But we had to say no, of course."

Louise still has the real estate listing from 1973. There's the black and white photo of the house, slightly shielded by "27 different types of trees;" measurements of the 10 rooms and the one-acre property; the names of schools and the nearest parish; plus annual taxes. Built in the 1920s, it had large windows facing Chatham Road. And in the top right corner, the listing price: $80,000.

Days later, just for fun after an outing to get a Christmas tree, they drove by Joel's house, and turned into the long driveway. And that's when they got stuck in the snow. The following week Fran called saying, "He's got an offer already but they want to tear down the house for an apartment building. He wants to sell to a family. Make an offer."

So, over peanut butter and jelly sandwiches (Bob always got home for lunch), they came up with their best offer which Bob declared "couldn't be a penny over $45,000 including closing costs and taxes, Louise!"

She vividly remembers phoning "my face red" to make the Ralph family's offer. And Fran's return call saying "you've got the house!!" And their move-in date: February 22, 1974 – Washington's birthday.

Louise and Joel's house at 1775 Chatham

Which is where Joanie picks up the story, with ever-bright memories of children "thick as thieves" armed with paint cans and brushes, listening to the Radio Mystery series as their parents stripped paint to expose the beautiful wood trim in the dining room and front foyer. Her dad died soon after that decade-long project ended.

"I was 16 when we put an extra bathroom on the first floor, and added the only shower in the house," Joanie reminisced. "Before that, we washed our hair in the kitchen sink!

"I remember the smell of garlic bread in our big house. My mom and dad had no money but they had a regular date night together. We'd all be banished upstairs and they'd settle in with a grasshopper or Manhattan cocktail before their meal of steak and potatoes.

"Not many weeks went by that Mom didn't remind us 'this house is a gift.' We were always aware of being very blessed in that house."

Here's a brochure I found listing Joel David Eastham as one of 14 members of the Boy Scout Pilgrimage Committee. The annual pilgrimage, started by Joel and others to mark the 150th anniversary of the birth of the 16th president, honors the trek that Abraham Lincoln took from New Salem to Springfield. "Both my dad and my brother earned the Scout's Order of the Arrow," Susan said with pride. The Scout's website notes Arrowmen "provide cheerful service to others."

In the Remarks section of the real estate listing Louise has kept safe all these years is the notation that the dinner bell in the back yard does not stay. Like Bob, Joel was a numbers guy, the assistant treasurer of the Chicago, Illinois and Midland Railroad. "That bell," said Susan, "came off a train engine that was going to be scrapped. Dad really liked it a lot, but he had no place to put it when he moved into his apartment by the State Legislature!"

It's the very bell that called the nine Ralph children to dinner from their games in the adjacent cornfield long ago. The bell that Louise's 29 grandchildren ring at every family gathering. Some Eastham family traditions – that bell, kids laughing, baseball in the big yard, flowers – thrive on the Chatham Road property today.

"Dad was devastated after Mom died," explained Susan. "We remember him saying how much he wanted a family with children to have the same experience we did.

"His gift to the Ralph family wasn't a one-time occurrence. Dad's whole life was about generosity really. He happily shared flowers and vegetables from our garden with neighbors; he served his country in WWII; he not only volunteered with the Boy Scouts but also with the Shriners and the First Methodist Church."

Like Abraham Lincoln, Joel David Eastham and his Muriel are buried in Springfield's Oak Ridge Cemetery surrounded by trees and bushes and history.

It'll be a swell film one day. And Robert will have to be good. Real good.

Before we left Louise last July, we took a few photos to remember her smile and the house linking two families, and the tangible proof that gracious generosities are all around us. For the wide shot of the house, Emmett and Liam walked with me down the yard while Louise sat on the top step at the front of her house.

Hugging each of us before we drove off,

Louise pointed at the street numbers by her front door. "Across the years, we've never forgotten Lisa and how connected she is to this house, too. She died at age 17 in 1975. Our address is 1775."

I think of Joel's house as a very real player in the Eastham and Ralph story.

I imagine the house watching in hopefulness for Louise's family that winter day, watching for a family of eleven. The exact number of big front windows still framing Louise on her porch.

GENROZT

I think my brother John has a big heart because he plays catch with me. He gives me cool pens. He wrestles with me. He helps me with my homework. He plays football with me. He loves me. He watches the kids at recess. He gives me shots. He watches us when Mom and Dad are not home. He plays with us in the pool in the summer. He plays in the snow in the winter.

Ryan D. 1st grade

Mr. B. is nice and generous because he brings us things when we work hard on things we do in school. He brings us ice cream and he draws and writes funny things. He makes us laugh and he is really nice. I think Mr. B. is a generous and cool person.

Celeste J. 3rd grade

One day I was in E.D.S. It's a service at our school that watches kids whose parents work late. I asked Mrs. W, the woman that works E.D.S., if I could get a drink of water from the water fountain. A kid from kindergarten comes up and asks me to tie his shoe for him. So I tied his shoe and then he said "Thank you" and walked away.

Seamus F. 6th grade

5

DALE'S COMRADES
generosities of heart, of comradeship, of community

My Mom, Rita Margaret Ena Maria – she of the gorgeous smile and feisty spirit – taught me to appreciate well-written obituaries as an excellent way to meet interesting people. Which is how Capt. Dale Noyd, USAF, came into my life along with the many generosities that followed him during and after his court martial.

His *New York Times* obit was titled "Dale Noyd 1933-2007 *Pilot Objected to Vietnam War*." Something his son, Erik, said made me put Dale's obituary in a folder with 15 or so others I hold onto. He said "[Dad] kept two certificates on the wall of his study .... One was his commendation for heroism, the other his dishonorable discharge."

Now, I'm not much of a military guy. I admire great-uncle Bill's serving in WWI, the WWII service of my Dad and his brother, Roland, in the Canadian Armoured Corps, and my niece Meaghan's year at the Royal Military College. I've visited Arlington National Cemetery in D.C. and I continue to study the U.S. Civil War, now in its sesquicentennial, even to writing about the 1861 Union training camp four blocks from our Des Plaines, Illinois, home. I've grown to appreciate integrity and honor wherever they're found.

You might be as intrigued as I was that an officer would hang his commendation and his dishonorable discharge side by side like equal honors. That inspired me to write to Erik three years after Dale's death to ask how I might know his dad better. And Erik's response led me to the trail of generosities that came into the captain's life triggered by his 1968 court martial.

First, some backgrounds.

My brothers and I are still known far and wide as the Silver Seven. We had exceptional parents named Bill (top salesman for Colgate-Palmolive) and Rita (vivacious, stay-at-home mother) who were engaged in our lives and engaging in their styles.

Dad was a reader at Mass at St. Gabriel's and a dynamic Christopher Leadership public-speaking instructor; Mom was a writer of challenging letters to newspaper editors, and one-time president of our parish's Catholic Women's League.

They taught their seven sons to stand up straight, look the other in the eye, and never quit. Mom coached us on human expectations with "You can't give what you don't have." And leaving the house, the last thing we'd hear was "Remember who you represent, boys!" Blessed indeed.

In 1968, the year Dale was court martialed, I graduated from Brebeuf Jesuit College School and went off to the University of Toronto focused on getting essays done and meeting up with new friends. That year my college, St. Michael's, had many more freshmen than usual from the States. It was a confusing, promising, maybe-we'll-finally-get-this-right time to be 18 years old.

Dale graduated 13 years earlier in 1955 from the ROTC program at Washington State University. His *alma mater* had produced CBS broadcaster Edward R. Murrow '30, who helped bring down Senator Joe McCarthy, and Laurence J. Peter '63 ("People rise to the level of their incompetence"), and bitingly funny cartoonist Gary Larson '72 of *The Far Side* fame. Not too shabby.

Apparently, Dale did so well in ROTC that he was the only one of his group to be given a regular Air Force commission right away. As a fighter pilot, he received a medal and commendation for successfully landing his damaged, nuclear-armed F-100 fighter at an English airfield. Later, he took a Master's degree in Psychology at the University of Michigan and then was assigned to teach cadets at the United States Air Force Academy in Colorado.

In 1966, Capt. Dale Noyd became one of the first military personnel to openly question America's involvement in Vietnam when he asked to be allowed to resign his commission or be classified as a conscientious objector. Not a surprise to learn that he was court martialed, found guilty, sentenced to a prison term, and dishonorably discharged.

Erik's gracious reply in Spring 2010 led me to many generosities starting with the small Quaker college in Indiana that had hired Dale Noyd. "Earlham," Erik wrote, "was a symbolic and literal life preserver for Dad and our family".

Since Earlham was en route to Peter at The Ohio State University, Erik encouraged me to stop as I drove east. "Dad's thirst for knowledge, passion for reading and unwavering dedication to the pursuit of justice ran through his veins as a life force," he wrote. "Glimmers of that could be found in students, flush with energy and seeking their passions."

Before setting out, I contacted the Quaker college that hired an ex-fighter pilot and heard from Dr. Nelson Bingham who had team-taught a psychology course with Dale. He's the provost now, and he hooked me up to Dr. Mic Jackson, a math professor during Dale's last few years at Earlham.

In one of those astounding ironies, Mic told me he was an Air Force cadet when Dale taught at the Academy. The reflection Mic wrote on hearing of Dale's death started with "Dale Noyd changed my life" and continued:

"When I entered the U.S. Air Force Academy in 1965, I had never heard of Vietnam. However, by the end of my first year, I was getting letters from a high school classmate who was seeing heavy combat in Vietnam with the Army's 82nd Airborne Division. I assumed our country was doing what was necessary to stop the spread of communism in Southeast Asia.

"In the first semester of my second year, I was fortunate to have Captain Noyd as my instructor for Introduction to Psychology. Captain Noyd had the reputation of bring a very good teacher. But more importantly, at least to young cadets who had visions of flying some of the best aircraft in the world, he had been an F-100 Super Saber pilot before being assigned to the Academy .... His class was my favorite that semester.

"One day during the following semester, our superintendent (comparable to a college president) called an emergency meeting of the Cadet Wing, all 2,000 students, [and] explained that Captain Noyd had been forced to leave his position on the faculty because he was a coward, unwilling to accept a combat assignment to Vietnam.

"I was shocked by the superintendent's words, turned to the cadet beside me and whispered, Captain Noyd is no coward. Those words initiated a personal journey that eventually led me out of the Air Force and to a career as a professor at a small Quaker liberal arts college."

In a second irony, Mic met Capt. Dale Noyd 18 years later when he was interviewing for a teaching job at Earlham.

"Dale told me that he had discreetly asked for another assignment because he believed that the United States military should not be involved in Vietnam .... Dale also told me that two upper class cadets had voluntarily spoken on his behalf at the court martial, risking their own careers ...."

Mic concluded with, "I am thankful that he stood up for what was right, but Dale Noyd paid dearly for his insight and courage. Thank you, Captain Noyd."

I liked that Mic signed off not with the rank he went on to achieve in his military career but "Cadet Squadron 02, Class of 1969," as Dale's long-ago student.

So with all this in mind, I arrived at Earlham a few weeks after receiving Erik's "life preserver" letter to be greeted by colorful Adirondack chairs, swings on tree branches, and parking spots with no meters.

Before we left for lunch with Phil Norman, another of Dale's colleagues, Nelson handed me his favorite memento from Dale, a wooden bust of Socrates, the constant questioner.

Over carrot soup and chicken casserole I learned Phil had arrived for his Earlham interview the same day Dale did in spring 1969.

Five years later, Nelson was hired to teach a curriculum Dale fashioned blending psychology, sociology and anthropology. It was called *Person in Nature, Society and Culture* and is considered part

Nelson with Socrates, his memento from Dale

of Dale Noyd's legacy at the college.

I met two more of Dale's friends that afternoon, comrades who spoke of Dale with warmth and generosity. One was his former student, Dr. Stephanie Crumley-Effinger '77, now a professor of religious studies. She recalled someone once saying Dale had "an eloquent life" and she added "his faithfulness – despite the consequences – formed me." The other was Mic Jackson.

On his office wall, next to his copy of the U.S. Constitution, hung Mic's high school reunion photo with him and buddy Larry Csonka (yes, that one, the great fullback of the undefeated 1972 NFL Miami Dolphins). Then another surprise greeted me. Mic took down from a bookshelf two Air Force Academy yearbooks, the *Polaris* of 1966 and 1967. Knowing that Dale's son would not have seen the 1967 book, Mic generously offered to give it to Erik and inscribed a message.

As I drove west to Chicago, the radio brought a third Dale-related irony. It was the 35th anniversary of the fall of Saigon ending U.S. combat in Vietnam.

The day after Saigon fell was Dale's 42nd birthday, May 1, 1975. He was finishing his first year teaching the new psychology course he helped create at Earlham. A future colleague, Mic Jackson, was resigning from the Air Force, his 1967 Academy yearbook carefully notated with 'gone' next to the names of 11 classmates. Frost's poem*The Road Less Traveled* was on the first page. I think Dale would have smiled at that.

On his 42nd birthday, Dale could have counted the generosities of his Quaker college among the best gifts he had, a community of listeners focusing on the pursuit of truth, respect for the consciences of others, and rigorous integrity.

Still, I had to find an earlier generosity in Capt. Noyd's life, the young cadet who testified at his court martial. With the help of Academy alums Mic '69 and Steven Simon, Lt. Col., USAF (Ret.) '77, current liaison to Academy graduates and donors, I did. Charles H. Heffron, Jr., M.D., USAFA class of 1967, was about to retire from his OB/GYN practice, hailed as one of Washington State's best doctors. Beyond irony, in a truly Dickensian twist, Chuck's medical office was a few miles from Erik's home!

At the Academy, Chuck wore #14 as a defensive back for Air Force and was president of his graduating class. On graduating, the future flight surgeon went to the University of Michigan Medical School, where a letter found him. It was from his Academy psychology teacher, Capt. Noyd, asking Chuck to be a character witness for him at his court martial in Clovis, New Mexico.

"It was a very amazing week for the people who were there to help Dale," said Chuck, remembering how Dale's team of ACLU lawyers had brought diverse witnesses to the area's only hotel. He spoke of the hotel's little bar with a fireplace where "seven or eight of us got together every night, me a first year medical student talking with the president of Georgetown University! It was a week's worth of amazing evenings."

So, I asked him why, exactly, did Charles Heffron, Jr., that 22-year-old cadet graduate, say yes to Dale possibly jeopardizing his career?

"I was in the 9th graduating class," he replied.

"Our squadron was like fraternity brothers. I wouldn't trade it for anything. Knowing the character of the person asking you was key. And Capt. Noyd's character was so strong. It never crossed my mind that I was taking my career in my hands."

Another supporter in Clovis was Charlotte Doyle, a fellow Michigan grad student, now a psychology professor at Sarah Lawrence College in New York City. Dale's panel consisted of ten officers, she said, all of whom had served in Vietnam, so the guilty verdict wasn't surprising. But at his sentencing, they allowed testimony about Dale's humanism "and the panel leaned forward and listened, obviously affected," recalled Charlotte. "It was one of the most amazing events of my life."

Capt. Noyd could have been sentenced to five years, but he was given the minimum, one year.

In a way, a way that a psychology professor might appreciate, the officers on his court martial panel could also be numbered among Dale's generous comrades.

GENROZT

At Christmas time my uncle and I decided that instead of getting presents we donated the money to India so that the kids could eat for a year. I felt happy for the kids.

Paddy B. 2nd grade

My grandparents own a restaurant. There is this homeless lady that always comes. She has very little money so my grandparents charge her only a dollar and sometimes give her the food for free! There is a lady who works across the street from the restaurant and she helped the homeless lady too. She let her stay at her house for a couple days. The homeless lady told my Mom that she got to shower at the lady's house. She said it was the cleanest she felt in years. This is my favorite generosity memory because not everyone has homes or families and we need to help them because they are like us. They suffer every day.

Sophia S. 6th grade

"December 1868
St. Nicholas Hotel, New York City

By this time two years I can so arrange all my business
as to secure at least 50,000 per annum.
Beyond this never earn ... make no effort to increase
fortune, but spend the surplus each year for benevolent
purposes ... no idol more debasing than the worship of
money ..."

from *Andrew Carnegie* by Joseph Frasier Wall

6

MISS OLA'S DIPLOMAS

generosities of heart, of many dimes, of hope

Chicago's grid system of alphabetically ordered streets is one of this area's best assets. For example, you can drive east from our house into Edison Park along Touhy knowing that Oleander is next to Olcott, which is next to Osceola.

You should know that my secret desire, every time we take that drive to Sheila's cousins' home, is to stop and tape a small photo over the letter 'C' so that it reads OSEOLA.

I'm pretty sure there are rules against that.

But that's how I'd like to honor Miss Oseola McCarty one day. With a photo of her smiling, lined face transforming the street named for a great Seminole chief into one honoring an elderly black laundry lady. You might want to remember Miss Ola and her diplomas the next time you're driving through towns named Osceola in South Dakota, or Iowa, or Arkansas, or Michigan.

This is why.

After more than 70 years of earning her living by taking in laundry in her hometown of Hattiesburg, Mississippi, in June 1995 Miss Ola donated her life's savings of $150,000 to endow scholarships for needy students at The University of

Southern Mississippi.

She is "an icon of generosity" as one of her 29,700 Google results says. Among those references, you'll come across the September 1997 gift of $1 billion that media magnate and CNN founder Ted Turner made to the United Nations. You'll read that his gift was inspired, in part, by Miss Ola's.

Notwithstanding the Internet, I keep newspaper clippings. Here are the ones I started gathering about Miss Ola the year of her gift, ones I've used in my work, singing the praises of Miss Oseola McCarty as I move among nonprofit organizations.

On a brightly colored sheet I hand out an August 16, 1995 editorial about her in *The New York Times* titled "The Gift of a Lifetime." Their phrase "the heart behind the gift" is the key phrase, I think.

On the reverse is a large photo from Cleveland's *The Plain Dealer* newspaper of June 7, 1996, showing Miss Ola, in cap and gown, receiving an honorary degree from Harvard University. Next to her sits fellow recipient Walter Annenberg, who gave Harvard $25 million, and to the University of Pennsylvania $125 million. I like that the heading over their photo reads, "Honored for her generosity."

The final clipping at the bottom of the page is from the October 11, 1999, issue of *Time* magazine. It's a 12-sentence eulogy by the very first USM scholarship recipient, Stephanie Bullock, ending, "I hope to live a life comparable to hers."

So, to prepare us for the rest of Miss Ola's story, the chapter that keeps resonating long after her death, I asked USM's help in contacting each of the 27 recipients of Miss Ola's scholarship through 2012. Swiftly and graciously, VP Bob Pierce offered to help, adding that many others were so inspired by Miss Ola's fund that it had almost doubled in the first few years. (Bob's emails end with "Southern Miss to the top!")

Some things you've just got to do. So I did.

Happily, I heard back from Miss Ola's first recipient, Stephanie Bullock Ferguson 1996-1999, and one of the most recent, Marauo Davis 2006-2010. Most folks refer to what Miss Ola did as The Gift. Here's how her diplomas are at work.

Stephanie's degree was in Business Administration; she graduated with a double major in marketing and management information systems. Then she went on to graduate school at USM, graduating in 2000 with an MBA and an emphasis on management information systems.

These are Stephanie's insights sent to me last December:

"Wow....where do I begin. My entire time at USM was filled with excitement. My four years of undergrad and one year of grad school were absolutely amazing. I never in a million years would have imagined that college could have been so awesome in every way. It was a wonderful period in my life. Because of Miss Ola's gift, I was able to graduate debt free! I am now 34 years old and I have many friends who are still repaying student loans.

"But, perhaps, I should just start at the beginning.

"I still remember the day we saw the article in the *Hattiesburg American* about the laundry lady who had donated a portion of her life savings to USM. We were all sitting around in the den, and my mom noticed the story. She mentioned that it would be a blessing if I could get a scholarship. Who knew it would actually happen just a few weeks later!

"I was preparing to go to work when the phone rang. It was the Foundation from USM. They asked me to stop by the next day in between classes to talk about me becoming a recipient of the McCarty Scholarship.

"I was just a freshman. A professor and some other people had mentioned me but I never found out exactly where my recommendations came from or why I was chosen. But sometimes that's just how God works, you know. Truly, truly a blessing.

"Shortly after that I met Miss Ola for the first time and fell in love! She was absolutely incredible. She was so authentic. She really cared about my education and about me. We immediately adopted her as one of our family.

"My grandmother (Mrs. LeeDrester Hayes) and my mom (Mrs. LeeDrester Bullock) were the ones who first taught me about compassion and generosity and how important it was to be grateful for all things. They emphasized the magnitude of being a sincere follower of Christ and getting a good education. It was no coincidence that Miss Ola fit into our family so well. It was destined.

"The foundation I received at home is what made The Gift life changing. I could have accepted the gift, had my tuition paid, and never talked to Miss Ola again. But that's not what The Gift was about. It was about love in its purest form.

"Miss Ola gave her hard-earned treasure so someone she didn't even know could have something she had always dreamed of, but was never afforded the opportunity to get: an education. Unconditional love like hers is going to be the theme of my book, one day.

"Miss Ola's gift resounded around the world and it brought out the best in most people. For me, it was a blessing to see people treat Miss Ola like a celebrity ... She dined with President Bill Clinton, she was on Oprah. Miss Ola and I did photo shoots for magazines, and speaking engagements. It was an exciting 15 minutes of fame. I even got to be on the *Today Show* with her. That trip to New York was my first time on an airplane, I remember.

"You asked me how I grew because of Miss Ola's gift. I grew in every way possible. My heart grew and my experiences grew. My horizons were broadened for sure. Most importantly, however, it was the lifetime impact that I will never forget. Miss Ola was the personification of the phrase, 'nothing is impossible.' She showed me that you can accomplish anything. She helped me to grow in my faith and it is my faith that guides every aspect of my life to this day.

"After getting my MBA I moved to Atlanta in September 2000 for a job with then-Anderson Consulting, now Accenture. In a nutshell, as an IT professional I test software but tons of other things go along with that. I am working on a very exciting project testing what is going to be one of the biggest technology trends in the very near future.

"In 2003 I married a student I met at USM, the most wonderful Lamar Ferguson. We have two beautiful sons, Cameron, 22 months, and Kylan, 7 months. My husband and I are givers by nature. We do our best to help whomever we can with whatever we have. We aren't rich, but neither was Miss Ola and she impacted a nation, a world!"

When I caught up with Marauo Davis 2010 USM, he was in his second year of PhD chemistry and biochemistry studies at Texas Tech University. He apologized that he didn't have much time for our phone conversation since he was heading back to campus for an evening lecture on analytical chemistry (go ahead say it; that's exactly how I felt too).

Marauo (pronounced Mare-ee-oh) graduated a semester early from his high school in Waynesboro, Mississippi, a one-hour drive from Hattiesburg. So he was able to start his undergraduate studies at USM in January 2006 with warm memories of a group of teachers, especially his 10th grade biology teacher, Larry Shoemake. "My parents said Go, it'll all work out and I started at USM knowing nothing about the McCarty scholarship."

"I remember walking back to my dorm after a calculus class and reading an email from a lady at the Alumni House inviting me over to talk. My high school counselor, Ms. Diane Fowler, had recommended me for the scholarship, I learned, and they were offering me full tuition and everything.

"I was in awe. A huge burden was lifted for me and my family. It was a really big break for us!

"Math and sciences had always been my love; I took college-level math in grade 10 so I jumped right into it at USM with professors like Dr. Lee and Dr. Holder.

"I remember Dr. Debra Booth encouraging me to think about doing research work. Inorganic chemistry is my primary focus and materials chemistry is my sub-specialty. I'm interested in studying 3-D, porous, nanomaterials, synthetic design and application of these in alternative energy processes."

Beyond his studies, Marauo serves in the Chemistry Graduate Student Organization and is the co-president of iSAMs, a group of students bridging the gap between the University's main campus and its medical school. His favorite non-academic author is Eric Jerome Dickey, who grew up in Memphis, got a degree in computer system technology, and worked in the aerospace industry before becoming an author and creating his globe-hopping character, Gideon, and writing 17 books, last count.

Marauo reflected on how the spirit of Miss Ola informs his studies.

"When I was on the USM campus I would talk to people about opportunities for them, about ways they could get involved. Through the McCarty Foundation, I received many opportunities, so I would watch out for others who were in need."

He was one of a dozen undergrads chosen for a semester-long program to prepare students for graduate school. That scholarship program was named for Dr. Ronald McNair, a scientist, saxophonist, and astronaut who died in the January 1986 Space Shuttle explosion. Marauo was grouped on a team with Simone Faulkner, whose undergrad studies were in communications and public relations. They soon learned they both were McCarty scholarship recipients.

Fittingly, the name of their grad school preparation team was *Challengers*.

Reflecting on what Stephanie and Marauo have done with their diplomas, so far, I'd bet Miss Ola is "happy as an angel half full of pie," as a guy named Timothy B. Doe once put it.

In her children's book *The Riches of Oseola McCarty*, Evelyn Coleman describes Miss Ola's reaction to her honorary degrees and awards, White House visit and Olympic torch carrying: "She used her new window air conditioner only when she had company. She shopped carefully. And she still saved her money."

Ted Turner was interviewed around the time of his 1997 gift to the UN, telling Larry King: "You have to learn to give. You're not born to give. You're born selfish."

If he's right, Miss Ola was an exception to Ted's theory.

In a USM story published as her donation was announced, she mentored all of us in generosity when she said: "I can't do everything ... but I can do something to help somebody. And what I can do, I will do. I wish I could do more."

The truth be told, Miss Ola is The Gift.

GENROZT

I was genares by making a very special picture called secrt squril for my dad's friend Tim. Tim asked me to draw it so I did and he was super happy that it came out perfectly and beautiful.

Christine S. 2nd grade

I went to the Big Ten tournament in Indianapolis. There was a person with a sign that said 'I am hungry.' I saw she was pretty old. A lady saw her and she went into a Subway and bought her a drink, sandwich and chips. She sat down, ate it with her and called her family.

Ely G. 5th grade

At my school there was a fundraiser for St. Jude's Hospital. I thought about all the kids who are sick and sad. I wanted to do something big. Our school's goal was whichever class had the most pennies would win a dress down day. I had forty dollars saved up. But my Mom wouldn't let me give it all. Even five dollars is a good amount. I hope that I helped someone out. I thought about how I would feel ... that's why I donated.

Christiana K. 6th grade

"I believe it is a religious duty to get all the money you can, get it fairly, religiously, honestly and give away all you can ... My opinion is that no man can trust himself to wait until he has accumulated a great fortune before he is charitable. He must give away money continuously."

from *Love and Money* by John D. Rockefeller
in *The American Story*

7

MADELEINE'S MISSION
generosities of heart, of mentoring, of a life of service

Looking back, I realize I wrote my letter of appreciation to the nuns who've touched my life just a few weeks before 9/11. This is what I wrote:

Today, I write to confess that I have been in love with you, forever.

All my life, surrounded by six brothers plus Wild Bill (now St. William 1919-1992) I have been in love with intelligent, disciplined women with great hearts and beautiful smiles. I have Rita (currently St. Rita 1921-1990 – just as she told us she was!) to thank for that pattern.

I have been remiss for too long in writing this letter... to thank you for saying YES! to that persistent call so long ago, for weathering the trials (me included), for responding to your every thin letter/obedience envelope with faith. And sweat. For struggling with the shards of other possibilities that hovered post-Vatican Council...

Always, always I have remembered you.

When I was nine years old and delivering morning papers to patients in St. Mary's Hospital at the top of our street in Kitchener (where four of my six brothers were born), I loved stopping at the chapel and there, among the few patients, seeing the Sisters — nurses in white, administrators in black – each with a snug wimple framing her face.

In that same year St. Francis of Assisi opened its doors with Sister Patricia as principal and her twin sibling, Sister Margaret, as music teacher.

Those were the first individual Sisters I fell for, backlit by the Advent wreath lighting ceremony when the whole school would line up, class by class, down the aisles that formed an "L". We had no gym, no lunch room. Just large spaces to run and Sister Margaret to bring us back with reminders about double beats, whole notes, and rests.

Years later I heard about a theory of music which holds that rests are just as much part of the music as are notes. Some of you to whom I write today are now rests; some of you are notes.

My 8th grade teacher was Mother Consolata, principal of St. Gabriel's in Toronto (a community infused with the one-of-a-kind Father Paul). I'm certain she saved me, the diminutive class president, from impeachment!

Through my high school years, I was harangued and inspired by priests – Holy Ghost Fathers from Ireland, and Jesuits from everywhere – and exceptional lay teachers like Les Luka and E.J. Barry. Our all-boys Brebeuf Jesuit was near the all-girls St. Joseph Morrow Park. In our final year, some of us wanted to continue Latin, and a few of them wanted to take physics and so we crossed Bayview Avenue for one (1) co-ed class per day.

The ever-smiling Sister Mary Augusta was just under five feet tall. For us, she agreed to un-retire for one final year of retracing Caesar's steps through Gaul and Horace's steps through a full life. And, among the 15 Latin students, I was the fortunate one to be assigned the desk immediately in front of Sister Mary Augusta's. Touching hers, in fact. To my query, she would just smile that beautiful smile of hers and insist that I already knew why.

And then there were the nuns on the faculty of St. Michael's College at the University of Toronto, particularly Sister Geraldine and Sister Frances. The former taught Spenser's *Faerie Queene* and, as months rolled along from bower to bower, I learned Sister Geraldine was taught by Sister Mary Augusta too!

I can conjure up Sister Frances's light, knowing laughter even now as she explained Chaucer's *Canterbury Tales* in a sweet Middle English accent. She particularly liked "The Nun's Priest's Tale" and that rascal Chauntecleer. Her joy became my joy.

In recent years I've been working among independent schools. Sister Bernard (her dad's name) Marie hailed from a city with both her congregation's Motherhouse and a federal prison. A physics teacher, Sister would speak of how back in the day the Sisters weren't allowed to watch basketball games in person, so they would take turns peering through the gym's movie projector portal.

When I met Sister Margaret Sue, she had been teaching 2nd graders in the Mississippi Delta for almost 40 years since opening the obedience envelope that sent her south. What a powerful impact she had at the inaugural for the new schoolhouse presenting handsful of dirt – each from a separate spot on the old property – telling us of the spirits that were in that good earth.

Her school was among the programs overseen by the singular Sister Maria Vincent, who was joined by two dozen Sisters from as many congregations. Like everyone else, I was felled by Sister Maria's smile and her probing, Socratic questions delivered in her southern lilt.

During Sister Maria's 50th anniversary of vows-taking, I listened to stories of how she was once passed over for a principal's role by a bishop who disliked her pink pantsuit and earrings; of how she sat forward, in another bishop's office in India, and asked leave to be bold so that land would be handed over for her Sisters work. And it was.

You are never far from my active memory, Sisters. And you will be there in my eternal one too.

I'll be honest with you. In the decade since writing that letter, I've dreamed of one day entering a ballroom and finding every one of my Sisters there and asking each if I might fill out her dance card. Sister Mary Augusta – *mirabile dictu* – would be first.

I learned so much more about Sister Mary Augusta's life of generous service on a visit to the headquarters of the Sisters of St. Joseph in Toronto. It was Canada's Remembrance Day, 11.11.11.

Sister's surname was Murphy, and she was one of eight children raised by Elizabeth and James just outside the nation's capital, Ottawa. She attended St. Joseph's College at the University of Toronto during WWI, finishing with second honors in modern languages and history.

Her examination results were published in the *St. Joseph Lilies* of September 1918, the same month her brother, Frank, was killed in France. Under her graduation photo are listed her Chief Charms (sincerity, wit, sympathy); Successes (scholarship every year and Italian Prize in freshman year); Achievements (Pres. of Tennis Club, Treas. of Women's Student Council, St. Joseph's Rep. for the Year Book) and a quote, *"Let others hail the rising sun!"*

If you Google that line, you will find that it's the opening of an 18th century poem by David Garrick on the death of a beloved English statesman, beginning:

Let others hail the rising sun!
I bow to that whose course is run

And further on you come to ...

Thy bosom glow'd with purer heat;
Convinc'd that to be truly great,
Is only to be good.

It hit me that she was using Garrick's ode not to mark her college years but to honor her dear brother, Lt. Frank Murphy.

Eerily, I read the name of my great-uncle, Pvt. Wm. J. Gearin, in the March 1919 issue she edited. It was listed among soldiers who sent thanks after receiving Christmas boxes from alumnae. A link, decades before we met!

She joined the Sisters of St. Joseph at age 25, the year U.S. women got the right to vote, and received the habit – the black and white outfit she wore to class with us 46 years later – the next year, in August 1921. Hey, maybe she took "Augusta" from that month!

Sister Mary Augusta lived a week beyond her Diamond Jubilee Celebration. Among archived documents was Sister's obituary, endearingly authored by a nun who knew her well. It reads:

"Sister's long years of service lay in the field of secondary education ... teaching for forty-six years in various high schools of the Congregation" and the names and dates of schools follow – among them St. Joseph's College School, St. Patrick's, and my other *alma mater,* St. Joseph's Morrow Park.

"During all these years she challenged her students to excellence, gained their confidence and respect not only because of her expertise as an educator but also because they saw in her a friend, a confidante, and a religious in touch with the world and its changes and problems to whom they could turn for guidance."

O, yes.

"Her warm-hearted humour and wit lightened the lives of those whose lives she touched forging at the same time many deep and abiding friendships. Sisters will recall her contribution of clever and witty poems and songs composed for Community celebrations over the years.

"During her eleven years of retirement she was a patient in the infirmary at Morrow Park. She was not one to complain of her frailty and while her activities were greatly curtailed she did not lose her interest in people, events and Community. All formed part of her apostolic life of prayer."

All this brought me back to my visits with Sister Mary Augusta as my college years came and went and I returned to Morrow Park to visit her. Our meeting spots graduated from the spacious waiting rooms off the convent's main lobby, to the small sitting room on her floor upstairs, to her infirmary bedside. We would talk about schoolmates, and family, and the plight of the Toronto Maple Leafs who, as a few of my brothers know too well, last won the Stanley Cup a season before I met Sister.

Sister Mary Augusta! C.S.J.

On one visit I boldly asked what her given name was and she confided it was "Madeleine." That started her into a delightful memory, reminiscing about being the youngest of six sisters. She smiled that gorgeous smile of hers recounting how one of them once told the young Madeleine that the robin on their windowsill had arrived just to sing to her.

Just this summer another one-time high school Latin student of hers, Sister Janet Fraser, told me that Sister Mary Augusta's "buddy" in her final years was Sister St. Phillip, a woman of dry wit. Sister

Janet summed up Madeleine's mission – and that of all kindred spirits – saying "it is a privilege to be invited to serve."

I've added Sisters Janet and St. Philip to my dance-card list.

My Sister Mary Augusta is buried north of Toronto in Holy Cross Cemetery, just across the way from where my parents rest. Her simple headstone reads:

Sister Mary Augusta C.S.J.
Murphy
June 29, 1980

Me, I would have added an exclamation point to her name.

GENROZT

The most generous thing someone has ever done for me comes from my Mom. When she found out she was pregnant with me, she was a 29 year old unmarried woman, not looking to have a child. My Mom always told me, even though she was worried, scared, and somewhat embarrassed inside, that she always knew it was a sign. "I wasn't worried about anything but partying. God was trying to tell me to stop." My Mom stuck there by my side through thick and thin. My Mom has always been my best friend since as far back as I can remember. For awhile, she had to play the role of a mother and a father to me. Now, being 12 years old, I understand how great of a mother she has been to me, and that is how I want to be towards my children.

Alisa F. 6th grade

One day my Dad and I went to a party, but we got there about a half hour late. When I got there they were all playing Monopoly. I asked if I could play, but they said there were already too many players. I went in the backyard bummed out. Then five minutes later one of the people playing Monopoly came out and asked if I wanted to play catch with him. I said yes, and he went to his car and got a football. We played catch almost the rest of the night laughing and saying jokes.

Stephen C. 7th grade

8

NORMA'S TRACKS

generosities of heart, of service, of an estate

When I first met Norma, she was four numbers, the first three totaling $79 and the fourth $1.3 million. As tickled as my new colleagues were by that fourth number, her stunning estate gift to our social services agency, no one knew her. No one. Her database information was sparse: an address, husband Bobby who pre-deceased her, and three small donations, the most recent 25 years earlier.

Like you, I know there are bushels of thoughtful individuals among us, going about their lives with empathy and skill, generosity and heart, largely unaware of the impact their gracious acts have ... almost invisible in our world.

So, I set out to make visible this unassuming couple who lived on Glenwood Avenue in Joliet, Illinois. Seven years later, this is the story of Norma and Bobby Benson, at rest side by side in Elmhurst Cemetery facing the morning sun with railway tracks running nearby. And not just any railway tracks. It's the Elgin, Joliet & Eastern Railway, the EJ&E, the one they both worked for and loved.

Norma's attorney, Lawrence Varsek, set me on my path to making Norma and Bobby flesh and blood again, if only in words. He had slim biographical insights, however. They were members of First Presbyterian church in Joliet; both were buried from the same funeral home with, as Norma requested, no wake and a short service attended only by their pastor, lawyer, and funeral director.

"Mrs. Benson was a very private person, a member of the Plainfield Historical Society. She was keenly interested in attending lectures on a variety of subjects as well as theatrical and musical performances ... " Bobby lived out his final years in one of two nursing homes. Lawrence recalled the day Norma made her bequest to that Illinois-wide social services agency. "She used to volunteer at a nursing home, I recall."

"As for that estate gift amount," he concluded "they were normal, middle class Americans I'd say. Their assets included a small investment portfolio, mutual funds, their railroad pensions, some CDs and savings, and their 1,100 square foot home."

Perhaps gratitude for Bobby's care inspired Norma's estate gift? Or first-hand appreciation as a volunteer for how that place touched the lives of residents and visitors? Norma didn't say. She just planned.

Norma Parvelescu (1930-2004) took courses in business at DePaul University in Chicago in the late 1940s learning typing, stenography – short-hand squiggles that looked like hieroglyphics – and office procedures. She got along well with her colleagues as a steno/clerk in EJ&E's freight accounting department which is evident when reading her chatty employee magazine columns which I found on the Joliet Historical Society's shelves.

Norma was one of three dozen Contributing Editors to the *J-Milepost*, each from a different department. Her column was named "The Revenooers," a pun on her group's revenue functions. The Gary Mills mechanics update was under "Bolts and Volts," the South Chicago clerks under "South Breeze," and the editors – both Roberts – under "Bobbin' Around." A fun environment.

Here's Norma in the November 1959 issue telling readers, "KEN CLARK hit the jackpot when he placed a dime in a telephone booth and got $2.20 in change!"

Farther down, after weddings and birthdays and a few illnesses, she writes "It was an honor for VICKI ONDRAK and family to attend the Investiture of the Cappa Magna, an honorary cape presented by Pope John XXIII to Rt. Rev. AMBROSE L. ONDRAK, Abbot of St. Procopius College, Lisle." Her words wrapped around three photos of EJ&E families. She ended with, "While in New York VERA ROSS had the privilege of meeting celebrity Groucho Marx and also drinking 'Irish' coffee." I love that touch.

Three months later, in the February 1960 issue, we learn that Norma was one of six women from EJ&E to attend the Railway Business Women's Convention at the Greenbriar in White Silver Springs. (The VERA who met Groucho went too.) I swear Norma has to be in the group photo on page 20.

The *J-Milepost*'s longtime associate editor was Robert J. "Bobby" Benson who took photos, wrote articles, and probably assembled those many Contributing Editor columns. Which is how he and Norma would have crossed paths.

Bobby (1915-1999) is remembered as a bright, fun man who always had a pipe in his mouth and camera slung on his shoulder. He was short, maybe five feet. His name doesn't appear on many articles, the lot of being an associate editor.

The first time I found them linked publicly is in the June 1970 *J-Milepost*, taking up fully one-third of Editor Bob Schiek's column. Under the heading "Associate Editor Forsakes Bachelorhood," we read:

"What could be more appropriate for this page in June than a wedding story, probably the first such news item ever carried on page three of this publication.

"On the afternoon of Saturday, May 23rd, *J-Milepost* Associate Editor Robert J. Benson and Steno-Clerk Norma H. Parvelescu exchanged marriage vows in a double ring ceremony held in the Memorial chapel of First Presbyterian church in Joliet... Attendants were Dr. Richard C. Benson, brother of the groom, and his wife Mrs. Vera

Benson. A dinner for immediate family was held at Al's Steak House following the ceremony.

"After a brief honeymoon the couple now resides in Joliet's west side. Bob and Norma plan an extensive wedding trip later this year. Your editor joins with hundreds of others in wishing them years and years of happiness together."

Reading that, you and I know Bobby and Norma were special. He was 54, she was 39 in June 1970.

Most *J-Milepost* issues had letters to the editor, some writers telling of meeting up with old colleagues on a trip, others complimenting the editors ... everyone sounding like family. In one of the letters four months after their wedding announcement, we get this memory of the young Bobby. It's from Charles Saiko at his new California address saying, "extend my best wishes to Bob Benson ... I remember him as the 'soda juggler' from Stillman's old drug store in Joliet."

The monthly timing of the magazine was changed that year, with a tell-tale clue in John Gleason's police department column in what was a November/December issue: "BOB and NORMA BENSON are back home after a two-week vacation. They both had a wonderful time and say Hawaii is just beautiful."

In seeking other voices, Attorney Lawrence Varsek steered me to envelopes that arrived after

Norma's death, which is how I contacted Chuck Hill, retired and now living east of Nashville, Tennessee. He was happy to reminisce about the couple he knew across 30 years.

"Bobby Benson was a very small man in stature but a very big man in his heart," said Chuck. "He was hardly ever without a pipe in his mouth. He loved the Masonic organizations – especially the Shriners. I have photos with him as he traveled to Chicago with our 19 buses loaded with handicapped children to attend the Shrine Circus each year. He never missed a one until his health gave way ... They made quite a picture together since Bobby was so short and Norma was quite a bit taller ... they don't come any better than those two."

Chuck laughed at an especially warm memory. "Early on, Bobby was in the parade's Clown Unit. He rode one of those small motorcycles but wrecked it one year!"

Now, like you I've come across a few clowns in my days: mine include the hairy-ankled CEO who refused to wear socks to meet with donors; the president whose Queeg-like antics made folks wince and wonder at her; the pontificating adviser who lionized himself daily, as he shaved; and, OMG, that martinet VP of HR. Bobby Benson only acted like a clown.

"Bobby was a character. Very bold and outgoing," continued Chuck. "He and Norma would help out in the many fundraisers I got involved with. When he walked into a room he stood out. He was a little on the cocky side, I guess, and said his piece at any meeting he attended. I remember one meeting when Bobby was talking and the guy next to me leaned over and said, "that's our entertainment for the day!"

Chuck remembers Norma as an unassuming lady. "She was very intelligent, which you heard in her vocabulary. She was laid back, shy, determined. Norma had love for people."

Before we ended our conversation, promising to toast the Bensons when we eventually meet up in Nashville, Chuck reflected on generosity. "People with hearts in their work give so much. A lot of people want the credit, but Norma and Bobby wanted no credit for all they did. They set a standard to go by.

"I was in their very modest Joliet home a few times. I like to read biographies of men and women to find out how they did what they did. It's great that you'll bring Norma and Bobby's history alive. It's unbelievable the estate gift they left."

Fittingly, Norma and Bobby's final puzzle pieces come from railroaders.

In his book about the EJ&E, co-author Ralph Eisenbrandt acknowledges the help of libraries, historical societies, and retired "J" employees and there, right there on page six, he thanks Bobby and

Norma Benson. Even better, the cutline below a photograph on page 20 reads: "Yardmaster Tom McLaughlin surveys the action ... Bob Benson had a great photographer's eye for a dramatic railroad photo."

When I telephoned him, Ralph explained, "the reason why we did that book was to honor those railroad people. We didn't want a book of photos of trains. It's about the people who ran the trains, who ran the railroad."

Ralph is an outgoing man, president of Unit 116 of the Joliet branch of the National Association of Retired and Veteran Railway Employees, most of them from the "J." Inviting me to their monthly lunch at the Silver Spoon on West Jefferson, Ralph told me to watch for his Jeep, license plate MCRR 1. That's for the Michigan Central Railroad where he spent his career. "When I started – my seniority day is September 4, 1956—a guy told me that every young boy should have one of two jobs: either a paper route or working on a section gang."

I told him I was a morning paper boy, long ago, but would gladly try my hand as a gandy dancer. Google that. Go on.

One of the six railroaders at their October lunch was Lee Graham who worked for the "J", most of his 38 years as a lineman covering 57 miles of track. "That's me on page 62 of Ralph's book. That photo was set up and taken by Bobby Benson. A cat named Tiger had been on a pole near the tracks in Park Forest, Illinois, for a few days. So Bobby set it all up, got me to rescue the cat, and put us on the front cover of the August 1964 issue. I tell my friends that I'm in the Library of Congress since Ralph's book is!"

Another railroader stopped at page 113, the photo of three men on Engine #668 freshly painted red, white and blue for the 1976 Bicentennial (even in black and white, it's a great shot!). One of the three was sitting on my right, trainmaster Willard "Buzz" Carey, 91, his walker out of sight.

Buzz served in the Railroad Battalion during WWII. "I left the "J" to join the army in June 1941. Six months later, on December 7, I was in a California town buying oxfords to wear home on my first furlough. I finally got to take that furlough three years and nine months later in August 1945!"

As my chicken sandwich arrived, Buzz announced that a girl he once dated, Vera, became Bobby's sister-in-law when she married Dick Benson, the dentist.

Sitting to Buzz's right was Jerry Harvey, 93, the senior railroader present. He, too, had left his job on the "J" to enlist. He was wearing a baseball cap with "USS Borie DD-704" on the front. "That was the last American ship hit by a kamikaze attack. We lost a third of our crew that day, August 9, 1945."

Jerry recalled how Bobby Benson was "like a general" when taking group photos. "At my retirement he gave me a bunch of photos he had taken with me in them over the years," said Jerry. "Very thoughtful guy."

In front of me is the EJ&E archive map showing the tracks that expedited freight traffic around the Chicago area, connecting as many as 30 different railroads.

The tracks form an arc from Waukegan in the north near Lake Michigan, southwest to Elgin, then east to Joliet, and a straight line on to Porter, Indiana. Just like its name said.

"People with hearts in their work"

Our city of Des Plaines has three railway tracks crisscrossing roads with nary an overpass. (At our Historical Society, led for decades by the irrepressible Joy Matthiessen, you can buy a "Blame it on the train" pin.) So I was hopeful that the tracks two blocks from our home would be Norma and Bobby's EJ&E.

Nope, they're Ralph's MCRR.

Still, we connect to the generous spirits of Norma and Bobby most days just a few blocks west of the tracks. It's when we drive along Graceland Avenue.

GENROZT

I was visiting my Aunt Jane and Uncle Frank from San Francisco. They came in for a week and their hotel had an indoor pool. We were getting ready to leave because it was way over my bed time (I was 7). As I was getting out of the pool my Mom asked where my sister Macy was. I looked around and there she was trying to stay above the water in the deep end. There was another family in there. As soon as their 9 year old saw Macy, he expertly dove to get her. He brought her out safely. We went to thank him and his family. They couldn't understand us because they didn't speak English.

Max K. 5th grade

Generosity doesn't have to be a huge thing. [A student's dad] is one of the most generous people I know. Every morning in the hall he says "Hello, what a nice day it is" or "How are you?" And when I won a writing contest he says "Congratulations, Bridget!" It is the little things that count.

Bridget D. 7th grade

9

GLADYS'S BEARS
generosities of heart, of time, of listening, of million$ also

Every time we speak of Miss Gladys and her generosities, my youngest sons Emmett, nine, and Liam, six, say that her best gift was listening. Which says a lot, considering she left millions of dollars to help sick children.

The first time I met Gladys Holm was in an August 1997 *New York Times* article. You might have read it too: *'Teddy Bear Lady' Gave Her Heart, Plus $18 Million*. It tells us that the smiling, smartly dressed Gladys in the photo "turned small opportunities into a giant legacy to a hospital."

Her boss, Foster G. McGaw, standing next to her in that photo, started a hospital supply company before the Depression and hired Gladys as his secretary. Across the years, Gladys invested wisely in stocks which grew and grew in value. Not even her closest friends knew how wealthy she was.

Still, as my guys say, her greatest gift was listening. This is how.

As a retiree, Gladys would distribute plush teddy bears to kids at Children's Memorial Hospital and, voila, their parents' financial worries would disappear. In her will, she left the largest gift that hospital had received up till then. The largest before that was $10 million from Ray Kroc, who built his first McDonald's about 10 blocks from our Des Plaines, Illinois, home.

The paragraph about her living in a modest townhouse in Evanston yet owning a king-size, red Cadillac sang to me. (Sheila and I were married in Evanston, and I still treasure the wire wheel covers from my 1969 yellow Cougar convertible.) Gladys and me.

So, after telling gazillions of nonprofits about the singular Aunt Gladys, a few years ago I caught up with the niece mentioned in that article. Dr. Lynne Adrian is chair of American Studies at the University of Alabama. She laughs a lot whenever she talks about Gladys. Lynne was 10 when she learned that "Aunt Gladys" wasn't her aunt-aunt, but an unmarried neighbor who took a special interest in the Adrian family.

Lynne's parents, Louise and Frank, met at Bell & Howell, the company that made movie equipment. She was born in Brooklyn in 1951 with a congenital heart defect that made her lips and fingernails turn blue when she cried. Soon after, Frank transferred to the company's Chicago headquarters, which brought them to Dr. Joseph Potts at Children's Memorial. As a toddler, Lynne underwent "the Potts procedure, moving my ribs to insert a shunt to take pressure off the heart."

She spoke as a veteran of many Dr. Potts visits including EKG and chest checkups. "I have this vivid memory when I was seven or eight years old," recalls Lynne, "and the wonderful techs were assuring me that it wouldn't hurt, and then I explained to them how it worked!"

Anyway, Lynne figures that her dad's upbringing had a lot to do with Gladys joining the family circle. Frank Adrian was the baby in his family, blessed with older sisters "so he collected maiden ladies like others collect stray cats" Lynne told me, laughing. Dinner tables often had 12 place settings including ones for their neighbor, Gladys, and her father, David, whom Lynne called "Pa Holm." Gladys listened to family stories and, just like with our family and yours too, I'll bet, that's how a caring friend became Lynne's "aunt."

Over the phone she described Gladys as an "outspoken, large-boned woman almost six feet tall" who grew up on a Christmas tree farm in northern Wisconsin. Years later when the farm was sold, Gladys brought the family's organ to her Evanston townhouse, and transplanted a fir tree to the backyard. (It's still standing today, maybe 40 feet high!)

Gladys graduated from Chicago's Lake View High School in 1928 and, for the next 41 years, was secretary to the founder of American Hospital Supply. By the time she retired, the company was the largest distributor of healthcare products in the world, eventually merged into Baxter International.

"Growing up, I heard how the young Gladys pounded the pavement looking for that job," recalls Lynne.

The only ostentatious thing Gladys got herself, not counting the large cocktail rings she wore, was her car. (If you Google "1967 Cadillac" you'll learn that Joan Crawford, the actress, owned one too, but she didn't drive hers to visit hospitalized kids like Gladys did.)

Lynne described her aunt's car in loving detail: "Gladys had long legs and loved the comfort. It was red with white side panels. And fins! It had a cherry red and white leather interior."

Gladys gave that car to one of her caregivers with three conditions: her estate would restore it; the Cadillac would follow the hearse to the cemetery; and, in farewell, the car was to be driven around her block in Evanston one last time. "She adored that car."

Lynne reminisced about her aunt's 80th birthday party, which she threw for herself in a nearby hotel. About 200 attended, some flown in by Gladys from Norway, one of the first times friends got a hint of Gladys's wealth. "I drove up for the party from Alabama with my kids," said Lynne, "and it was a regular Auntie Mame three-ring circus. She sure had zing!" That day, Gladys announced she was endowing a lecture series at Northwestern Hospital.

Lynne told me about her aunt's collections of

spoons, hundreds of them hanging on racks on her walls. And Franklin plates, especially of Elvis. And Lladro china, including a scale model of Michelangelo's *Pieta*.

"And, of course, her teddy bears."

You can hear the smile in Lynne's voice as she envisions Gladys, always sitting in her favorite recliner, surrounded by beautiful, squeezable teddy bears lined up on her couch, all of them gone when Lynne next visited.

"None of us had any idea that Gladys collected teddy bears to give to sick children – and their brothers and sisters – to befriend them and to hear how their family was doing. Then, magically, hospital bills got paid. I didn't know till 20 years later!"

As our conversation ended, Lynne reflected on her aunt's generosity.

"Gladys heard how much my parents worried, and saw how I spent so much of my young life waiting for a heart machine. She saw the impact that heart research and medical people at Children's Memorial Hospital had on my life.

"When I was in my 30s I remember how much Gladys wanted me to come to Chicago and go with her when she made her preliminary gift so that Children's would know it was occasioned by Frank and Louise's daughter."

Only after her death did Lynne learn about

the $18 million estate gift from Gladys to support research on heart diseases.

"In a funny way, I found her gift tremendously freeing. As a person with a congenital birth defect you can develop 'survivor's guilt' I guess you'd call it. Gladys's gift meant that I didn't owe what my years of hospital care cost. I could just repay with my support and experience."

With Lynne's blessing, I contacted Gladys's estate attorney and, not long after, Dale Park welcomed me to his office to talk about his client "with the big smile and friendly personality." A slim, silver-haired gentleman looking like *Law & Order's* Jack McCoy hopes to look one day, Dale began with a few facts: Gladys was born June 25, 1909, and died at home June 18, 1996; her funeral had only a few attendees who gathered later at a restaurant across from the cemetery, just as Gladys planned it, to "talk about the good times."

"I write wills and trusts, that's all I do," Dale continued. "I remember someone contacting me and asking me to stop by to see Gladys. I remember stopping in front of her townhouse late one afternoon and thinking 'it's so modest, this will be pro bono.' Gladys knew exactly what she wanted to do.

"I remember her telling me how her boss would call the office early most mornings and dictate letters to her over the phone. And she would

Emmett, Liam and friends visiting Aunt Gladys

have them typed and ready for his signature – remember those were manual typewriters in those days – when he arrived. She worked hard all her life, with great affection for Mr. McGaw, her company, and that small group of men she worked with in her original office.

"Somewhere along the line," Dale recalled, "Gladys asked me to drive her Cadillac on trips to Children's Memorial. I'd push her in her wheelchair, and someone from the hospital pushed one of those canvas-sided bins, probably six feet by three feet, filled with teddy bears.

"Gladys would ask 'where shall we start?' and we'd go from floor to floor with Gladys giving away big, fluffy bears to any little child she saw, many with no hair, many in bed with tubes attached, their brothers, sisters, and frightened parents at their side."

Dale said visits would take 90 minutes to two hours. "It was very emotional. There was no frivolity, no talking as I drove Gladys home. I once asked why she undertook those visits, and she replied, 'because I love children.'"

As I drove away from my conversation with Dale, no word of a lie, the car in front of me at the first light had one of those special license-plate frames. It read: *Where kids come first. Children's Memorial Hospital*. Gladys again.

Just this summer, the hospital moved to a beautiful new building and is now called the Ann & Robert H. Lurie Children's Hospital of Chicago. They brought along the endowed fund created from Gladys's gift, a fund that generates annual dollars to underwrite research, targeted therapies, and novel treatment methods. (American Girl and Legoland stores are only a few blocks away now. Nice.)

Both Lynne and Dale told me to reach Lois Jebb, Gladys's next-door neighbor and longtime friend, and when I finally met Lois, we were chaperoned by a smiling, three-foot-high clown statue – a gift from Gladys.

Turns out Lois often drove Gladys to meetings, outings, and even a few Wisconsin trips in that red Cadillac. (Lois fancied white convertibles herself.)

Sitting next to me in her wheelchair, wearing lovely round earrings to mark our conversation about her good friend, Lois began, "you know, Gladys always seemed the same age. She loved her two cats, the outside one named Tigris, and her beautiful Siamese, Chingchong, who was handed on in her will, I think." She spoke of their drives to stockholders meetings; of Gladys's favorite drink, J & B Scotch; of Gladys's rheumatoid arthritis that slowed her down in her later years; of Lisa, the caregiver who inherited the Cadillac.

"The day Gladys died I was outside planting marigolds, I remember. Lisa called and said 'Gladys just passed' in her Southern way." Gladys's favorite flowers were roses, added Lois.

At the end of each of my conversations, I promised to visit Gladys, who rests in Skokie's Memorial Park Cemetery.

I like visiting cemeteries (Mom did too, wouldn't you know.) My youngest sons trundle along with me ... Liam working on his math as he scans the birth and death numerals; Emmett keen on the carved headstone designs. A few weeks before heading off to visit Gladys, we three spent a few hours in Chicago's historic Graceland Cemetery a few blocks from Wrigley Field. They still talk about one headstone shaped like a baseball, another shaped like a golden pyramid with a sphinx at the door, and Daniel "Make No Little Plans" Burnham's island.

So that we'd know Aunt Gladys before we found her grave that hot, sunny July afternoon, Emmett read aloud from that 1997 *Times* article as we drove. As he finished, we agreed that we should bring something special for Aunt Gladys since she was such a generous soul.

We checked a few stores but couldn't find any toy 1967 Cadillacs like the one Aunt Gladys adored, so Emmett recommended a flashy red Mustang. And Liam spotted a bandaged teddy bear, saying Aunt Gladys would love that too.

Emmett asked to be our navigator again, just like at Graceland Cemetery, and watched carefully as an employee named Tom circled a cemetery map indicating where we would find Aunt Gladys.

It was Section G (as in Gladys!) and after a bit of wandering, we found Gladys next to her mother Hilda and father David. Their names are etched side by side on a plain headstone.

The boys arranged the small car and bandaged bear we brought along. Looking around at the flowers on other graves, we figured it wouldn't break any rules to plant the small red Mustang. So we did.

Each of us said a few words of thanks to Aunt Gladys, then took the short drive to circle Gladys's block in our chili-pepper-red Saturn SUV. We liked that Gladys had lived across from a large park filled with families. Then off we went to lunch at the restaurant near the cemetery, the one where folks went to speak of the good times after Gladys's burial 15 years before.

In between bites of pizza and sips of lemonade in the sunshine of Zhivago's patio, Emmett mused aloud about the kind of person who was a multimillionaire but marked her grave with a simple, flat marker. "Humble," said Emmett. "Aunt Gladys was humble."

Best of all, the listener and giver who grew up on a Christmas tree farm is buried right next to a large fir tree.

GENROZT

My soccer coach helped me learn how to dribble the ball, and dribble around the other player, and also how to keep it away. It was very very very generous of my coach to teach me all of the stuff that you do in soccer. My coach also taught me how to be a goalie and how to kick the ball really really really really hard.

Mia M. 3rd grade

One of my favorite generosity memories was when a family that are friends of mine had a mass that was dedicated to my Great Grandma that died earlier that week. My family and I were so touched. Some of her friends and family came to the mass to help us get through the hard time. This is a very generous thing that the family did for my Great Grandma. I will never forget this memory.

Charles E. 6th grade

My favorite generosity memory was a time that really moved me, a moment I did not expect. And that moment was when a kid on my soccer team, who truly despised me because of jealously, put out his hand ... I had kept trying to keep him cool, but it came to the point he couldn't control himself, when he tried to fight me. But a week later, he came up to me, said nothing, and just put his hand out to me. Since then, we've been good teammates.

Michael P. 8th grade

10
HEROES LIKE MARY JANE AND IZZY
generosities of heart, of community, of teamwork, of lifetimes, of song

Sometimes I replay my *Highlights of Stephen's Life* stored in my long-term memory. You probably do this too, with your version of the little trophy you got as highest goal scorer when you were 10; that first kiss with a girl named Beverly; the drive to your first job in that blue convertible; the last raucous camping/canoeing trip with your dad and brothers; holding your first-born, and hugging him 25 years later; that afternoon in the Uffizi in Florence. My highlight reel has an audio track, too, with Earth Wind & Fire's "September" cranked way up.

You understand.

Which is why you'll appreciate my powerful, two-hour highlight from February 26, 2010, when Mrs. DeShon, in her 40th year teaching 1st grade, and Izzy Idonije, defensive end for the Chicago Bears, teamed up because one was named Teacher of the Month by a local university, and the other came to Our Lady of Destiny grade school as part of her celebration.

First, a word about Mrs. DeShon who, in fact, does have a first name. It's Mary Jane. When she graduated college, she thought about working at Colonial Williamsburg with all that history and architecture. But teaching youngsters became her vocation, so to speak, because her own 1st grade teacher seemed so mean and she wanted to change that for others.

And the next 40 years flew by for Mrs. DeShon and husband Art as she orchestrated Pig Days, and Flat Stanley reports, and pumpkin-patch outings, and Christmas pageants, and captained her young scholars in the wooden sailboat in her classroom where they sit and read.

Israel "Izzy" Idonije #71 started with the Bears as a practice squad player in 2003 and is a fan favorite – fans like our Mrs. DeShon and Mrs. Wetendorf. He was born in Nigeria and grew up in Manitoba, the Canadian province that sits atop Minnesota and North Dakota. Shortly before his visit, Izzy was the team's candidate for the NFL's Walter Payton Man of the Year Award recognizing "outstanding balance" between civic and professional responsibilities in the lives of nominated players. Izzy spends much of his off-season bringing shoes, medical help, and hope to children in Nigeria; in-season, he sacks quarterbacks.

On the February Friday Izzy arrived, Emmett, currently in 4th grade, was one of Mrs. DeShon's students, and I was there with my new digital camera. Here's a shot of Principal Linda Chorazy and Izzy as he ducks under a hallway banner that reads CARING, one of seven values that greet students daily.

Here's Emmett's buddy Auggie in his Bears jersey, and here's Izzy lifting up football-loving Brandon so he can mark Izzy's height on the classroom door frame. Check it out when you visit. It's still there.

Here's Izzy lying down on a roll of orange paper as Jane (the Packers fan present!) traces him so students can spend the year perfecting their math and measuring skills using his six-foot-seven outline. Here's Izzy, perched on a little chair, reading to students.

And here's Mrs. DeShon's keepsake photo with Izzy between her and Bears owner Mrs. Virginia McCaskey, whose children went to a predecessor school, St. Mary's.

Mrs. DeShon, Izzy, and Mrs. McCaskey that fine Friday in February

These and dozens more photos of Izzy's 1st grade visit capture a warm, funny, willing man surrounded by adoring children and a few smiling adults. But it's the second hour of Izzy in the gym with all 150 students that became the highlight-within-the-highlights for me that day.

The school had contacted Izzy's Canadian high school history teacher and football coach, Kevin Grindey, who wrote this reflection with humor and admiration. It was read aloud after a rousing student rendition of "Bear Down Chicago Bears'" with the ever-gracious Mrs. McCaskey sitting next to the piano:

"Did you know that before Izzy was a Bear he was a Viking?" Kevin wrote. "Before you get too upset please know that was the nickname of his football team at Vincent Massey High School in Brandon, Manitoba, Canada.

"Izzy's (or Iz ZED as we say in Canada) football career didn't start like most of the players in the NFL. Izzy didn't play at a big high school with artificial turf and a stadium. In fact he played on a beaten up old field that had more gopher holes than grass. There were so many holes that we used to get the injured players to stand in the gopher holes so other players wouldn't get hurt. There was no grass where Izzy played high school football – only weeds.

"Most NFL football players come from high school programs with years and years of tradition and history. Izzy's high school team was a new program that was using old and outdated equipment – we didn't even have enough game jerseys so some players had to wear practice jerseys during the games. The team didn't even play in a league; we only played six exhibition games.

"Izzy didn't play in front of thousands of people like they do in Illinois. At Vincent Massey we were lucky to have a few parents and a dog at our games (the dog usually cheered for the other team). Izzy didn't even play American football he played Canadian football where you get one point if you miss a field goal – how Canadian is that: 'Nice try on the field goal. You can have one point just for trying EH!'

"Izzy didn't play with or against kids that had been playing football since the time they could walk, who dreamed of playing in the Super Bowl. The boys (and one girl) on his team dreamed of hoisting the Stanley Cup, and they could tie up their skates with both arms tied behind their back. Izzy didn't even play football until he was in Grade 12 (he loved basketball) and it was his Mom that made him try out for a Manitoba all-star team after high school.

"Despite all of these odds, Izzy's hard work has led him to the NFL. His faith in the Lord, and his family, have kept Izzy on the right path. I believe that Izzy's kind and generous spirit is a gift from God. The NFL is only the platform that allows him to spread his gifts.

"Izzy's accomplishments on the field are great but it is his off-field commitments that really demonstrate the hero that he is.

"Izzy didn't just decide to help young people after he became a star in the NFL. Long before the bright lights of Soldier Field, Izzy was committed to helping people in his community.

"I first knew Izzy when he was a young volunteer at the YMCA. During his time there Izzy would brighten the day of countless children with his amazing smile and his giving heart (and his great voice ... ask him to sing an old camp song!)

"Izzy transcends all cultural, social and racial boundaries and makes all of the children he comes in contact with feel unique and special. To me this is a far greater gift than scoring a touchdown or making a tackle.

"I heard Izzy say once that if he was only remembered for football that would be a tragedy. I know that the legacy he is building off the field will long outshine his accomplishments on the field.

"I am very proud of what Izzy has done in football but it doesn't even touch the pride I feel when I see Izzy contributing so much to the communities he calls home. If we focus on just Izzy the football player we miss so much of who he is. We will fail to see the real impact he is making on the world.

"Not all of us will have the opportunity to play professional football but all of us can make a difference in the lives of others. This is what inspires me the most about Izzy and I hope that all of you grow up to be heroes like Izzy."

Students later reflected on what they learned that afternoon and their thoughts are also in the photo album we gave Izzy.

"You should always listen to your Mom." – 1st grade "You don't have to play football to be a hero. Never give up on your dreams. Don't waste opportunities. Get good grades." – 3rd grade

"Stay in school. It's better to be known for giving than winning. Live up to your dreams. If things go wrong, God is always there. If you're trying to do something always try your hardest." – 4th grade

"Izzy told us to always follow our dreams. Also he told us to try very hard and to never give up. Finally, Izzy sang us his campfire songs!" – 6th grade "Anything worth having, you have to work for." – 8th grade

You should know that when I replay those two hours of highlights from that day, I always include an invisible attachment. I imagine 40 years of Mrs. DeShon's voice, patiently and lovingly imparting the same things Izzy did. I conjure up her discipline and sensitivity bestowed one scholar, one day, one report card, one year at a time.

Happily, every now and again one of Mrs. DeShon's special efforts was captured, like the 2009 Christmas pageant, anchored by Emmett's 1st grade thespians:

Yesterday's one-night performance of the annual Christmas Pageant was an artistic tour-de-force for its 80+ performers, and another pearl in the long chain of presentations, in and out of her classroom, for its writer/director/producer Mrs. DeShon. In a word, scintillating!

In the tradition of Steppenwolf groupies festooned parents, grandparents, aunts and uncles and siblings – one brother of a 2nd grader sporting his Jonathan Toews Blackhawks sweater – scampered for the best St. Stephen pews a full 40 minutes before things got rockin' at 7 p.m.

Throughout the evening a Group of Five – 8th graders Jacob, Abbi, Julia, Raven, and Rosemary – delivered introductions of the unfolding birthday tale drawn from Bible sources plumbed by the writer. In turn, these words were enlivened in 13 well-rehearsed hymns by the beautiful voices of Christmas-colored-clad students from all grades (though, in truth, some of the pre-k types performed more as props than players; you know who you are, Liam).

This was the first time the entire student body would be on stage, choreographed cascading down the steps of the altar. At the center of this vignette were 27 1st graders, one of the largest troupes under Mrs. DeShon's direction in her years of overseeing this millennia-old story.

Among the hymns sung by angels-for-the-evening-and-maybe-longer were Gentle Woman, We Three Kings, and Twinkle Twinkle Little Star.

But the song the gathered multitude awaited – as it does annually – is the Ballad of the Christmas Donkey sung by the entire cast. This year's donkey, Bella, engagingly reprised the role her mother had also performed in an earlier DeShon Production.

A holy diorama of eight angels, seven shepherds, and five sheep supported the perennial three kings, as well as Mary, Joseph, and Innkeeper. Indeed, many in attendance were especially taken by the way Baby Jesus was lovingly delivered ... handed one-by-one through seven angels into Gabriel's hands and then on to His smiling parents. (Note: the Babe's weight and height measurements are yet to be confirmed as this review went to press.) Merry Christmas all!!

Thinking of the many gifts Mrs. DeShon brought to blossoming scholars and their families across four decades has me remember my beloved high school history teacher, E.J. Barry. He also taught English, directed plays, and coached hockey, a Canadian renaissance man. Emmett's middle name, Joseph, has him carry Mr. Barry's initials.

I remember particular teachers who have imprinted my sons: Matthew's Mrs. Berkowitz, and Peter's Mrs. Grabo, and Emmett's Mrs. Blanchard, and Liam's Miss Holderness. (Today, he's halfway through Mrs. DeShon's XLIIIrd class of 1st graders!)

As well, I remember the faces of educators marking my life decades after graduating university: leaders like Karl Ertle, Father Jack Kleinhenz, S.J., the Sisters Carol(e) Anne Griswold and Smith, both H.M., Jeff Leitch, the Gladstone brothers, Father Paul Cusack, C.P., and Pastor Bob Furreboe – all of them dedicating lives and hearts to dynamic future worlds.

Each of them generous heroes like Mr. Grindey and Mrs. McCaskey, Mrs. DeShon and Izzy.

GENROZT

I think Father Noel has a big heart. he came on a field trip. He also comes to are class room. He says mass on Wednesdays. He like to tees us. He is so funny too. He loves us!

Abigail B. 1ˢᵗ grade

Mr. Cutro, our Cub Scout leader, prepared a fun Tiger Cub Christmas party with games and crafts and story telling for one hour on a Sunday – all for just one Tiger Cub, my little brother Nate. He also included me in the party. He let me play too.

Augustus S. 3ʳᵈ grade

My favorite generosity memory was when my parents' good friend, whom I consider my uncle, gave me my first electric guitar. He fixes guitars and used to play in a band. Whenever I'm there he teaches me something new for guitar. The guitar he gave me he had for a long time. He was supposed to repair it for a customer, but the customer let him keep it. My uncle's son passed away not too long ago. His son – when he was little – had accidentally broken the guitar right after he fixed it ... so it has a deeper meaning for me.

Lauryn T. 7ᵗʰ grade

"Ingratitude is a failure to recognize the good things, the graces, and the gifts received ... "

"Teach me true generosity."

Saint Ignatius of Loyola

11

KIRSTEN'S SCOTT, HABIB'S BURSAR, STEVE'S NACHO MAN, AND PAT'S FRANK

generosities of heart, of action, of timing, of money, of mentoring

In preparing to write this book, I invited random folks to contribute their own GENROZT memory, the one that always brings along that joyful ache.

I met Kirsten Millet when she welcomed my eldest son, Matthew, into her 8th grade advanced mathematics class. Which was a generosity in itself! You see, as his year began, Matthew went to Ms. Millet to ask if he could move over from the general math class. She said yes; Matthew excelled; today he's a financial analyst. The power of yes!

"Running the good race" by Kirsten Millet

I have always believed that things are paid forward – what goes around comes around; get good, give good, get good ... Are you with me?

I have been blessed in my life with a wonderful family, supportive friends and excellent teachers from kindergarten to college. How do I pick a single generous act from one of my parents or my teachers? There were so many that did so much, and they all helped to shape my life.

I was running one night and thinking about a

defining moment and it hit me, and as I think back it seems so obvious. I have always believed people enter your life for specific reasons. Whether they are part of your life for short periods of time or long periods of time, they become stepping stones into the fabric of who you really are.

When I was young my mother and father were part of an organization known as JAGS. It stands for Jefferson Area Girls Softball. Our small farm town developed such a good softball program that our high school teams were known across the state. My father was the coach and my mother the manger of numerous teams my sisters and I played on. In high school I was blessed with enough ability to be a three sport athlete, so my schedule for games, matches and races was non-stop.

And every time I looked in the stands both of my parents were there. Always!

At college, when I ran cross-country and track, my parents charted their weekend routes so they could see every one of my races taking place in any one of maybe ten states. My college friends still tell stories of my mother yelling and cheering and my father running to the next spot to see me, his neck watch in hand, frantically glancing at my time. My father, Jon, is a numbers wiz who can calculate splits in his head faster than my TI-83.

Unlike many parents, mine never pushed or criticized, only supported. After college when my husband, Aaron, took over the role of street supporter at road races, my parents were still there. Like clockwork.

Then, about eight years ago my father was diagnosed with Alzheimer's. I remember the Cleveland Turkey Trot was the first race of mine he ever missed. As I write this, I'm 36 years young, and I still want – still need! – my parents at my road races. They have caught several over the last few years, but the differences are glaring: no watch around Dad's neck because he can no longer read the numbers or understand what they mean; no questions about age group, mile pace or splits; and when I finish, I can tell in his eyes, Dad's not quite sure what I have just done.

I'll admit it. There was a hole in my life that I refused to acknowledge. Until a guy named Scott began to fill it, unknowingly.

I am a track coach at the high school where I began my teaching career 13 years ago. One week out from our first official day of spring 2010 practice we were in desperate need of another coach for boys' and girls' distance running. We had feelers out everywhere and Aaron, who teaches in a nearby district, even asked the staff at his high school. One name came up.

My first phone conversation with Scott went well. I could tell by his spewing of numbers and knowledge of times and expectations that he exceeded the qualifications. When I mentioned he would be coaching girls as well as boys the phone fell silent; he had never coached girls before. Our meeting with Scott was on the first day of practice, and we wanted to escort him right from the interview to the track. He was perfect! Hired!

His knowledge of the sport gave him instant credibility, but his love for the growth of the individual athlete shaped our athletes' devotion to him. (Scott came to have a deeper affection for the girl's team ... boys do not bring you flowers at the end of a long run!)

Scott is a numbers wiz. Knows splits of athletes long forgotten, can calculate an ending race time based on a single repeat workout, remembers my license plate number, my birthday, and the record time I set in high school.

We ran at the same college, Scott some years before me. (Well, lots of years!) As runners we would share stories, and training frustrations, and he would listen.

At that time, the last road race I had won was in Pittsburgh, four years and three children earlier. I could not imagine getting back to where I was before. But Scott came up with the statistics of successful women runners my age. He began to offer suggestions for my workouts, then to discuss my running progression, and then wrote monthly workouts for me.

Scott suggested which races I should enter and what times I should be hitting. He phoned (does not text, yet!) to inform me of upcoming races and asked if I would like to run them together. I find myself thinking, "what would Scott say?" when I hit a mile repeat time that I thought was out of my reach. I had my own personal running coach!

Scott and his wife, Cindy, are part of our lives now. With open arms they have welcomed Bay High School Track and everything this new job has brought.

As I look back on our first phone call I remember hanging up the phone and saying to my husband, "this Scott guy acts like he doesn't know how to coach girls. I don't know if this is going to work." We've had a few laughs about that in the years since!

Well beyond the coaching he has brought to our athletes, Scott has filled a place in my life that I didn't realize I needed. He did not have to do any of this for me. I believe Scott was placed in my life for a reason, asking nothing in return. I thank God for him.

And I have a dream that one day – just maybe – my Dad and Scott will be able to share their magnificent love of numbers in a language all their own.

I met Habib Hosseiny in my fundraising role at a New Jersey hospital, just outside New York City, soon after I emigrated from Canada in 1985. He and his family are Baha'i, a faith that encompasses all religions with openness and equality and tolerance. Beyond tolerance, actually. Make that acknowledgement. We came together to help a singular family that fled Habib's native Iran after the 1980 Revolution.

"I will never forget .... " by Habib Hosseiny

After about 16 years of employment as a public school teacher of the English language in Iran, I decided to go to graduate school for a Master's degree.

Finally, my effort in obtaining admission to the School for International Training in Vermont came to fruition. It was a 12-month program for the Master of Arts in Teaching (MAT) degree. Our intention was to return to Iran after the program.

My wife and I decided to take advantage of the opportunity and brought along our children – then 12, 6, and 4 years. It was August 18, 1978, our son's 4th birthday, when we arrived in Brattleboro, Vermont.

A taxi took us to a beautiful motel and left. When I went to register, I realized that my small briefcase, which contained all of our passports and $8,000.00 travelers' checks, was lost!

The motel manager did not kick us out. We stayed that night – my wife could not sleep though. In the morning, my phone calls began, and I traced back to see where we might have left it. I hitchhiked, for the first time in my life, to the town where our plane had landed the day before. The briefcase was left in the taxi, and was returned to me untouched. I immediately called my wife and gave her the good news!

We rented an apartment and began our new life with a great deal of difficulty. The children started school where their classmates at first believed they were deaf and unable to talk. However, the problems in Iran diverted our attention.

Gradually, the revolution happened. Our relatives and friends advised us to try to stay because it was not safe to go back. Many of my Baha'i friends were jailed or executed. All the Baha'is lost their government jobs.

The school community in Brattleboro knew and understood my situation. The financial department offered that I should pay back the remaining part of my tuition in unbelievably low installments of $10.00 a month.

Then it was right before the Christmas and New Year holidays that the bursar asked me to see her. She gave me a $1,000.00 check and said it was mine. She did not say where it came from but indicated that I might spend it any way I wished. She repeated that I did not have to pay it back, but if I wanted, I could whenever I was able to.

I will never forget the generosity of whoever gave that money to me and my family. My prayers are always with that person.

Every now and then you bump into a kindred spirit or, as I say about Steve Cardamone, executive director of Lockport, Illinois's Give Something Back Foundation, you bump into him, get knocked own, come up laughing, and get knocked down again. You've met the type.

"Sometimes nachos can save a world"
by Steve Cardamone

It was probably 1985 and the venue was the Rosemont Horizon Arena, now Allstate Arena. However, it will always be THE Rosemont in our house. My mom and dad decided to make a dream come true ... the 12-year-old me was going to see my hero, Hulk Hogan, wrestle live.

I remember that night I looked at the "fight" card thinking, "I have to wait to see the Hulkster until the very end?" (In retrospect, I think we all wish we could enjoy the ride a bit more and stop worrying about the main event.) I lived a rather sheltered young life. I blissfully boast that point.

I had more opportunities to string together "perfect pieces of time" than anyone I have had the opportunity to share my life with since. Safety, happiness and predictability were hallmarks in my childhood and blessed is about the best word to articulate the journey. And it remains true today!

This is important for you to understand. Because that night, for the first time, I was asked to get some snacks for the three of us before we found the way to our seats. I am sure Mom was nervous to let me go (a metaphor for life!) but she relented. The real reason Pop was temporarily ridding himself of my company was to surprise me with a t-shirt and foam finger on my return.

As I waited in line (patiently, just like a big boy) I looked back and saw Mom and then focused on the task at hand: what to eat? I remember trying to project the image of a confident 12-year-old who knows exactly what he's doing. I ordered three Cokes and some nachos.

As is the case worldwide, I was confronted by a disinterested countenance with lightning-fast fingers on the cash register. I stood there in anticipation of the inevitable question "Are you buying this all by yourself?!" (An obvious opportunity for an adult to reinforce how far I had come in this world!) Instead, I got the dull thud of "That's 12 dollars." What, no trumpets? No, smile? And then, looking down, I experienced things James Bond never had: moist palms, sweat beading on my brow, and ears beginning to turn red.

I was looking at a 10-dollar bill.

These days, I would simply turn to the next person in line, make a self-deprecating quip about how I need to take some time to learn math, and ask the purveyor of terror to take one of the Cokes off the bill.

But that night, I froze. I looked down hoping that the $10 bill had multiplied. It had not. I glanced over my left shoulder. No Mom or Dad. Before I could look at my hand again the man directly behind me reached over my right shoulder, threw down two bucks, and said, "Have a great time tonight!"

I took my cardboard tray of sporting-event fuel off the small ledge and walked back to my parents. Pop had a foam finger on and was waving it with a smile. I explained what had happened at the register even as a cold shiver ran down my back from the sweat that was not yet dry. They asked, "Who helped you?" and I turned to point out the man but he was gone.

What do I wish I would have done? I wish I had looked at him. I definitively know that I said thank you, but that man's face should be in my memory. I was so embarrassed and surprised. He deserved to see the tears welling up in my eyes and feel my thank you ... more for helping me save face than the $2. (In truth, tears are streaming down my cheeks as I write this.)

He could have been a drunk, a rogue, a terrible father, but for 30 seconds, an angel. Is that not the definition of redemption?

Second, I wish I could let this man know – right now – that he changed my life forever. A simple act like his is often underestimated. But not by me! In a world where fundraising strategies abound, nothing is as authentic as a gift that needs no acclaim, with no repayment required.

When you grow up in a home where your dad is your hero – the man who could literally pick up a car, a man respected in our town – then living up to a certain standard is important. Because of a stranger's heart I averted a youngster's meltdown.

For decades I have been on the hunt for a particular opportunity: I have waited in many lines for someone ahead of me to run short of funds so I could let them know that sometimes, love can be simple, anonymous and highly impactful.

I have been close a few times, like at the grocery store once a woman — obviously flustered – unsuccessfully tried a few credit cards. I slowly reached for my wallet, my heart pounding like that 12-year-old again. (Will I offend her? Does she need the help? Is her family struggling to pay the bills? Is her card simply worn from use?) Finally the third card she tried worked, we exchanged pleasantries, and I lost an opportunity. My search continues.

So, if you are ever in line struggling for cash, and you break into a cold sweat realizing you are a wee bit short, do me this favor. Turn around.

If you see a tall bald guy with a grin on his face reaching for his wallet, let him pay, please. You will have given him the greatest gift of all. But, for Heaven's sake, let him look you in the eye!

I first met Patrick Benedict Kahnert when he was a few hours old. He was, as Mom announced, "my baby" and since I was being displaced in the family pecking order, visitors needed my permission to check him out. But for me being ungenerous and telling him "no" when he was a lad, this generosity story would never have happened.

"Frank Selke, Jr.'s autograph" by Pat Kahnert

For a language that is fraught with ambiguity and mixed meaning, two simple words can do so much to build trust, confidence and appreciation. Which is why I always say, "thank you" for a singular man's generosity in helping me get started in my marketing career. His name is Frank Selke, Jr.

The other day I was digging through some old files and found a letter that was sent to me when I was eight. The envelope was addressed to "Master Patrick Kahnert" at 80 Pleasant Avenue, Kitchener, Ontario (no postal code – which tells you it was some time ago!). And, the piece de resistance was its return address – Club de Hockey Canadien Inc., c/o Montreal Forum.

The note inside and an incredible attachment were the initial inspiration for my career, and a continuing inspiration in my life. Here's the story behind the envelope:

One cold winter's night, I got to join my dad and an older brother, Stephen, at my first Kitchener Rangers hockey game at the local arena. But my excitement was less about seeing the Rangers play than seeing one of my hockey idols, Dickie Moore of the Montreal Canadiens, drop the puck to start the game.

On the way to our seats, we bumped into one of Stephen's morning newspaper customers, an accomplished community leader, and he said he would get Dickie Moore's autograph. Even though Stephen was an avid Detroit Red Wings/Gordie Howe fan, and would normally have nothing to do with the Canadiens, he was excited.

For my entire young life I had been a Canadiens fan. So, I begged my brother to give me Dickie Moore's autograph when he got it. I even promised to get up every day at 5:00 a.m. to help him with his morning route for a next week, for a month, and – my final offer – forever.

At the end of the game, as promised, Stephen's customer handed over Dickie Moore's autograph. I remember staring at his little piece of paper with a burning desire to call it my own. That was not going to happen.

The next day at Mom's suggestion, I printed a letter to one of her Toronto childhood schoolmates who worked for the Montreal Canadiens. My note was to the point: "Dear Mr. Selke, Would you please send me a hand-autographed team picture of the Montreal Canadiens. Thank you, Patrick Kahnert."

The next week I opened a brown envelope with a note and a team photograph of the 1960-1961 Montreal Canadiens, another Stanley Cup year!

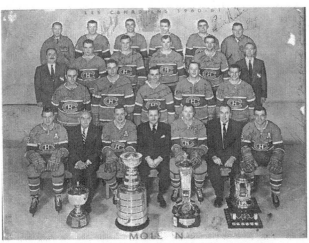

It was autographed in ballpoint pen by each of the players. My heart raced. There was assistant captain Dickie Moore in the front row, far left.

I no longer wanted Stephen's mere scrap of

paper. I took my autographed photo with me everywhere I went sharing my new treasure with friends. For three straight years of show-and-tell I blew my classmates away, and I am pretty sure it helped me become class president in Grade Six.

Even more valuable than that autographed team picture was the accompanying note, the first of a number of letters from Frank Selke, Jr. I kept in touch with him throughout my teenage years, and he kept responding, often along with a hockey picture. (We hockey fans never age.)

He always took the time to answer my letters, and my questions about public relations and business. He gave me honest feedback, and valuable advice on how I could prepare myself for a communications career: "read interesting books... write lots of letters and stories... work in the media... protect your reputation... be honest... follow your dream... work with people you trust... help others succeed... don't get lost among the glitter." And Frank Selke, Jr., achieved all of those!

You're probably wondering about my childhood treasure. The photo with faded tape marks and pinholes in each of its four corners now hangs in my son's bedroom. Every time I pass it I smile and my eyes find my friend, on the far right in the second row from the top. His autograph at the bottom of each of his letters is a lifetime treasure of mine.

GENROZT

I'm thankful for my Mom and Dad because they love me and they want to make sure I get the best grades here at O.L.D. I'm thankful for my foster sister. Hope we keep her forever. She loves us and we love her.

David P. 3rd grade

My favorite generosity memory is every single day I spend with my parents. They care for me, give me unconditional love, buy stuff, give me a home, and much more. They give up a lot of stuff for me too. I try to be the best son I can be to them and pay them back for all the stuff they continue to do. I love them with all my heart. They have great personalities and because of this they have made me who I am today. My Dad helps me with math homework all the time even though he could be playing piano. My Mom washes my clothes, makes my lunch, and cares for me whenever I am struggling.

Matthew M. 8th grade

READER'S MISSION:
NOW IT'S YOUR TURN

In preparing these chapters, I came across many stories about generosity.

Here's a reference to the Friendship Train that crossed the country in 1947 collecting food from American donors to needy Europeans; Emma Lazarus donated her "Give me your tired, your poor" poem to help fund the pedestal for the Statue of Liberty; Andrew Carnegie gave us free libraries nationwide a century ago, and Col. Jim Pritzker gifted us a unique Military Library here in Chicago a few years ago; Patsy Cline is loved as much for her generosity as for her crossover hits.

In 2010 Nick Sidorakis, captain of the Oklahoma State basketball team, gave up his full-ride scholarship so that other student-athletes could join the team; that same year an elderly Canadian couple, Violet and Allen Large, won an $11 million lottery and gave most of it away within a few months saying, "That money we won was nothing. We have each other."

In his book *14 Cows for America* Wilson Kimeli Naiyomah returns to Kenya from studying at Stanford nine months after 9/11. Maasai village elders are so moved at his story of tall buildings melting that they donated their precious cows to America "because there is no nation so powerful it cannot be wounded, nor a people so small they cannot offer mighty comfort." (A decade later, my godson Thomas, then niece Shannon, went to Wilson's Kenya as volunteers, the former to help build a school, the latter to teach at one.)

Then there are the generosities closer to home.

A few blocks from Sheila's Museum of Science and Industry (jump-started by a $3 million gift from Julius Rosenwald) is the *Mellow Yellow* restaurant, whose menu recounts how songwriter Donovan graciously allowed the use of his 1960s song title, at no cost. Our family's dental hygienist, Kunjal, cut her flowing hair to give to an organization that makes wigs for cancer patients; our hair stylist, Serena, is a regular volunteer with a community agency serving autistic children. And, miraculously, last fall Sheila's cousin Julie received a lifesaving gift of lungs, and all of us give thanks to that donor and family with her every breath.

The boys and I met up with Russell Spreeman who regularly tends the gravesite of "Pony Bob" Haslam, to honor the memory of the greatest Pony Express rider; our neighbors, the Kozlowskis, paid a sculptor to create a smiling bear out of the stump of their 100-year-old tree that had to come down, a joyful gift to passersby; and just last spring the folks at Nashville's historic Hatch Show Print generously welcomed Emmett to serenade their shopcat Huey in his musical world premiere. (Check out *Emmett, Huey and Sue* on YouTube)

Emmett with his guitar and precious wingman,
Liam, off to his world premiere

Your life has folks like these too, I'll bet.

A March 2012 article in *Psychological Science* told us: "genes that influence certain hormones contribute to niceness and generosity in people ... participants who found the world threatening were less likely to help others …"

In truth, I didn't need a study to tell me that people who are open to others are generous, and those who are closed are not. I learned that long ago from Rita and Bill, and saw it readily in Stratford's Tom and Toronto's Frank, Cleveland's Joan and Nashville's Kathleen. And so many more.

In my Introduction, I told you how brother #8 was folded into our family and, just like the rest of us, Mike found his way to the backyard at 26 Caracas Road to chat with Mom and Dad about girlfriends, baseball's Blue Jays, hopes, and life.

When Dad died in the summer of 1992, the eight of us carried him to be reunited with Mom, and Mike was in the middle.

We later gathered in Peter's yard for fine burgers, cold brews, and the usual Bill-and-Rita tales accompanied by loving asides and laughter. Pat brought along the blue Stetson that Dad had worn, rain or shine in all seasons, and it became the annual Spirit of Bill Award. Mike was its first recipient and wrote this:

> *To be named the first recipient of the award is an honour that may never be topped. The comfort that it brought me to be even considered and the joy of caring for the blue Stetson … a constant reminder that the spirit lives forever.*

And now it's your turn.

The detective fiction writer Raymond Chandler said, "A good letter is an act of generosity: it uses the voice its writer thinks with, the voice he talks aloud to himself with."

Write that letter to the one who imprinted your life with his/her act that still brings you a joyful ache when you think of it. Write it out.

Mail it soon, using one of the Post Office's beautiful stamps. It doesn't matter if your Sister Mary Augusta died decades ago, the one who opens your GENROZT memory envelope will be thrilled.

Then share it with me, please. You might have been the only person to behold that GENROZT!

The time has come.

To share your own GENROZT memory
and to contact Stephen:
www.generosity-GENROZT.com
www.facebook.com/generosity.GENROZT

If only Lincoln . . .

Artist – Matthew Stein

AFTERWORD

Dave Hilliard, President and CEO
Wyman Center in St. Louis and The Wyman National Network

Having the last word on a storyteller like Stephen Kahnert is an opportunity not to be missed. So, here it is: our always-bold storyteller is himself a paragon of that which he chronicles.

I know this because he has been both friend and professional colleague since arriving some 20 years ago as the consulting partner of a firm we'd hired to resuscitate a flagging capital campaign. We had begun it to raise funds to upgrade century-old Camp Wyman, which provided summer respite and hope to impoverished St. Louis children since 1898.

In that campaign and in prep for future ones, Stephen gave of himself far beyond what was required by the engagement. His gifts to us were belief in people, and the potential of what might be when visionary leadership and caring, competent people with generous hearts are set free. He taught, coached, inspired, motivated, planned and persisted in service to a mission that became his as much as ours. I watched him document the stories of generations of adults whose life trajectories had been changed by Camp Wyman. Their memories inspired the campaign and, as importantly, they lived anew a bit of their youth ... "a gracious act that created a joyful ache" in the remembering.

Stephen brought us words and ideas that helped us see ourselves as we might be rather than as we were then. He saw us leveraging our work beyond one historic camp to reach tens of thousands of youth each year. He said he could see us as an exemplar of the American youth camping movement, up there on the cover of Time, featured on CNN. He imagined patrons making million-dollar investments at a time when our annual budget was less than that!

Twenty years later, I can report he got most of it about right, though the magazine was *INC*, and it was NBC that chronicled our story of innovation and social entrepreneurship that has leveraged our camp programs into community and school-based services in 33 states, the District of Columbia and Ulaanbaatar, Mongolia. Today we reach more than 50,000 teens annually. And we've attracted multiple million-dollar gifts from generous, forward-leaning donors.

Who'd have thought it?   Stephen. (OK, he never thought about Mongolia.)

As I read through the life stories in these chapters, I've been musing on a few of the big questions about the nature of generosity.

I wonder … are we humans hard-wired to be generous like we're hard-wired with certain survival traits? Why the variations in the expression of generosity among people and across cultures? Is generosity an expression of our spiritual selves?

And here's what I believe: We all have the capacity for generosity, but its release requires cultivation and ignition.

For me, my first cultivation lesson was from my parents when I was six as they sent me to deliver a ham sandwich and glass of milk to a hungry hobo on our back steps. He told me that the strange chalk marks on our alley ash pit signaled others that this home had kind people who unconditionally offered a sandwich and respite. I watched my parents accept an African American boy into my previously segregated 1950s Cub Pack, welcoming him and his family, enduring vilification from narrow-minded others. Then my 16 years of education with the Sisters of Loretto and the Jesuits fueled the ethic of striving to be sincere yet effective in service to others. These were my igniters, my role models.

One of the most generous and happiest men I have ever known is Charlie Wells, a learning-disabled maintenance man at Camp Wyman for 30 years. He was a Depression-era kid from a dysfunctional Seattle family of 12 that rejected him and his disability in his teens, but he refused to reject them. Charlie became the distant, anonymous brother and uncle who funded Christmas and housing and used cars for people he never met but always loved. That was Charlie.

In his book, *Outliers* Malcolm Gladwell

addresses the sources of extraordinary excellence in all endeavors. It's about time on task, he says. Extraordinary performers achieve mastery through a minimum of 10,000 hours of practice. I believe Mrs. DeShon, Joan Southgate and Charlie Wells became Grand Masters of Generosity ... a virtue that wasn't just a character value but the spirit animating their lives.

I believe stories can translate mystery into meaning and ignite meaning into mattering.

In this collection, Stephen has presented us role models, a "storied" approach to our spiritual selves, and a means toward self-mastery. I say let's practice, practice, practice. We and our world will be better for it.

St. Louis, Missouri
September 2012

ABOUT THE AUTHOR

Stephen Kahnert, Generosity Coach, has cultivated a hybrid career across three decades in consultant and executive leader roles in fundraising – from mission reviews to volunteer renewal, strategic planning to executive searches, capital campaigns to major gift conversations – in addition to a decade in corporate marketing and the media.

An excellent listener, a dynamic team builder, and an accomplished motivational speaker, Stephen lives with his wife and the youngest two of his four sons in a suburb of Chicago.

Made in the USA
Middletown, DE
02 July 2024

56706663R00088